however, as consumers rush to ~~buy~~ ~~cheap~~ ~~American~~ personal computers, the company has seen its sales collapse. In a last desperate attempt to revive the fortunes of the firm, the CEO has called in the hard-nosed young Turks of **McVITIE CONSULTING** to restructure the company.

ITO is an office lady who knows that, if male chauvinism did not force her to spend all her time doing petty tasks around the office, she has the nurturing power to make Suzuki Denki a great company again.

■ McVITIE CONSULTING ■

WATANABE completed an undergraduate degree in Japan then went to business school in America to get his MBA. He is the founder and CEO of McVitie Consulting, a company with a mission to create ideal business solutions through a fusion of Western and Eastern values.

CHUCK is an American, and the only other member of the distinctly "lean and mean" two-man McVitie Consulting firm. Despite having worked in Japan for several years, there are areas of Japanese language and culture which still elude him. Advising Suzuki Denki is to be a learning experience for him.

INSTANT BUSINESS
JAPANESE

INSTANT BUSINESS JAPANESE

Real-Life Skills for Real-Life Situations

GILES MURRAY

KODANSHA INTERNATIONAL
Tokyo • New York • London

TRADEMARKS

Apple, *Newton*, and *Powerbook* are trademarks of Apple Computer, Inc.
Microsoft, *Windows* and *Where do you want to go today?* are trademarks of Microsoft Corporation.
Thinkpad, *Aptiva* and *Solutions for a small planet* are trademarks of IBM Corporation.
Prolinea, *Contura*, *Praesario* and *Has it changed your life yet?* are trademarks of Compaq Computer Corporation.
Intel Inside is a trademark of Intel Corporation.
The Network is the Computer is a trademark of Sun Microsystems.
You've got a friend in the business is a trademark of Gateway 2000.
Your trusted adviser is a trademark of Hewlett-Packard.
Pack-Mate is a trademark of Packard-Bell.
Woody and *Pronote* are trademarks of Panasonic.
Dynabook, *Rupo* and *Brezza* are trademarks of Toshiba.
Mebius and *Zaurus* are trademarks of Sharp.
Flora is a trademark of Hitachi.
Winbook is a trademark of Sotec.
Biblo and *Deskpower* are trademarks of Fujitsu.
Can Be is a trademark of NEC.

Distributed in the United States by Kodansha America, Inc., 114 Fifth Avenue, New York, New York 10011, and in the United Kingdom and continental Europe by Kodansha Europe Ltd., 95 Aldwych, London WC2B 4JF.

Published by Kodansha International Ltd., 17-14 Otowa 1-chome, Bunkyo-ku, Tokyo 112, and Kodansha America, Inc.

Printed in Japan.
ISBN 4-7700-2105-4
First Edition, 1997
97 98 99 10 9 8 7 6 5 4 3 2 1

CONTENTS
目次

はじめに

サラリーマンの"マインド"と言葉の分析

日本に来て2年後、私はイギリスに本社を置くある会社の東京支局に就職しました。その当時、私は学校でしか日本語を学んだことがなかったので、日本の会社の日常的な雰囲気について知識も経験もありませんでした。従って一般の外国人と同じように、日本のビジネス界についての先入観やステレオタイプにとらわれていました。日本人は皆、例外なく礼儀正しく、感情表現の穏やかな働き者だと信じていたのです。つまり、日本人のサラリーマンは仏様から授かった神秘的な力でもって、貿易業の僧として経済的な奇蹟を起こす人々であり、他人との軋轢のない、ただGNPを増やすための無味乾燥なロボットに近い存在だと私は思っていました。超集団主義、超資本主義の日本社会の中で、ひとりひとりの個性は経済成長に寄与・貢献しないものとして排除されてしまったのだと。

もちろん、実際に会社に入ると、良い意味でも、悪い意味でも、事実は私が持っていたイメージとは正反対でした。私が発見したのは「日本のサラリーマンは、他国の人々と全く同じように感情を持った、個性豊かな存在である」ということでした。

日本人のサラリーマンは決してユニークな存在ではない!

本書の目的のひとつは、私の実体験からの発見を皆さんに伝えることです。そこで、まず外国人の読者にも、日本人の読者にも理解していただきたいのは、西洋のビジネスマンと日本のサラリーマンの間には、違う点より共通点のほうが多いということです。ビジネスの最終目標は金儲けですから、そこへ到達するための行為、手段、考えに類似点がないということはあり得ないのです。

破壊された私の先入観、と新しい発見を具体的に以下に述べます。

礼儀正しい仮面も時々剥げ落ちる!

「日本人は、拷問をかけられても丁寧に話す。」

もちろん、現実上、デッドラインがあったり、ちょっと頭の回転が遅すぎる部下がいたり、クライアントに気難しい奴がいたりするようなことがあると、高いポジションにある人ほど想像以上に怒ったり、人をけなしたりします。礼儀正しいという仮面の剥げ落ちる一瞬です。

会社は素早いが社員ひとりひとりはトロイ！

「どんどん新しい商品を低価格で発売したり、外国のメーカーを倒産に追い込んだりと、世界の様々な業界を支配し、グローバルビジネス界で最も恐れられる日本企業においては、社員は皆決断力に富み、活発で自信満々なアクションマンに違いない。」

優柔不断を極める日本の社風を味わって、私ががっかりしたのは当然のことだと読者の皆さんには理解していただけると思います。

精密機器：粗末な口

必死になって「正確な日本語の表現を使わないといけない」と信じ込んでいた私は、＜こと＞、＜ところ＞、＜方向＞のようなあいまいな言葉が多いことにびっくりしました。また、日本人の営業マンは＜購買意欲不足＞などの専門知識を披露するような単語を無視して、＜消費者があまり買いたいと思わないという問題がある＞というような簡単な単語で構成した、長い説明的な文章を使っていました。最初は自分が騙されているんじゃないかと疑いましたが、最終的にわかったのは、大ざっぱな表現を使うのは、ネイティブ・スピーカーにとって自然なことだということでした。ここでは、母国語の名詞と外国語の名詞の1対1の置き換え、つまり単語と単語のブツブツ交換は機能していないのです。加工しすぎるのは外国人だけ。母国語とネイティブ・スピーカーの間の関係は落ち着いた、束縛のない結婚のような関係だと言えます。外国人のターゲット・ランゲージに対しての態度は、恐妻家の前で、またはお見合いの席で神経質になって堅苦しいことしか言えない男性みたいなものです。言葉は、多くの女性と同じように少しぐらいは汚されたり、苛められたり、けなされたりすることが好きなのです！

単一民族日本人は混血語をしゃべっている

私が抱いていた間違った考えに、＜日本人は日本語をしゃべる＞というものがありました。オフィスの現場で気付いた不思議な現象は、やり手のサラリーマンが脱日本語を実践し、和製英語を使いまくることでした。外来語は、格好をつけたり、コミュニケーションを効率的にする潤滑剤としての役割を果たしていました。学校で一生懸命に頭に入れてきた漢字の四文字熟語は、実際には誰も使わないのです。＜経営戦略＞は皆、＜マーケティング戦略＞と言い、＜恩恵を受ける＞は必ず＜ベネフィットを受ける＞か＜プラスになる＞に切り替えます。日本人は混血語に走り、純日本語を使おうとするのは外国人しか残っていないという狂った時代です。

迷わせるコ・ソ・ア・ド言葉

先の和製英語ショック以上に、言葉そのものの問題もありました。それは、ちゃんとした文章を使わずに、同一民族の日本人は以心伝心でお互いの考えを読み取ることが出来るのではないかということです。一生懸命文法的に正しい文章を目指していた当時の私は、「例のあれどうなった？」「ああ、あれねぇー」のようなコソアド言葉を初めて耳にした時、自分の努力はすべて無駄だったと痛感したのでした。日本語を使いこなせる日本人のサラリーマンは、言葉を超えて意味のないような片言で意見交換をするのです。なんと、代名詞とブーブー言う言葉（？）だけで通じるとは！これは日本のサラリーマンに特有のことです。私は何のために苦労して名詞、形容詞、接続詞、副詞を覚えたのでしょうか、情けない気分です。

＜退屈＝安心＞という不思議なマゾ体質

最後に、ミーティングとプレゼンでサラリーマンは、結婚式でスピーチをする人と同様に、説明力と自己編集能力に乏しく、長い時間に渡ってだらだらとしゃべりますが、これは全然犯罪視されていません。日本では人を退屈させ放題にできます。ビジネス界では、書類が簡潔に書いてあれば、人間の話す内容はいくらだらしなくても許される、ということのようです。

読者が受ける英語のベネフィット

（1）共通点を強調

日本人は日本にユニークな文化があるという神話を鵜呑みにしていますが、私の経験で判断すると日本人のサラリーマンと西洋人のビジネスマンの共通点は非常に多くあります。この本はその共通点をベースにしています。外国人の読者は私が提供する＜表現部品＞を組み立てることによって、自分らしい日本語を話せるようになるでしょう。日本人の読者は英語を話す時、西洋人に変貌する必要はありません。自分の日本人としての特徴（曖昧さ、戦国時代の武将へのあこがれ、物造りを金融より尊重すること等々）をそのまま英語に持ち込むことが出来ます。ですから、普段自分が一番よく使っている日本語表現の英語を丸暗記することに

よって、自分なりの英語を話せるようになります。インターネット時代、英語が通じない人はダメだとよく言われますが、私は、英語が通じるか通じないかということより、自分の英語が自分の性格を正確に反映しているかどうかが大切だと思います。

（2）厳選した超実用的な英語

この本に出てくる表現はすべて現在の日本のビジネス界に基づいたものです。私はマーケティング業界やその他いろいろな業界で活躍している会社とともに、プロジェクトを行った経験があり、この本の中の例文は、一つの業界に片寄っているということはありません。また、自分の経験や仕事環境（つまりフィールド・ワーク）だけに頼らず、2年間に渡って、ビジネス誌に掲載された日本を代表する企業経営者のインタビューを読み、日本のビジネス界で最も有力な人物が何を不安に感じているのか、どのような将来の計画を立てているのか、そしてどんな話し方をしているのかを深く研究しました。教科書によくある現実離れした表現はひとつも載せていません。また、日本人が好きなネイティブ・スピーカーでも理解出来ないほど、複雑な受験用の文章も載せていません。即戦力を与える、即席表現の供給を目指しています。

（3）狡猾に国境なし

多くの日本人が日本語にしかないと思うような曖昧な表現、間接的な言い方、つまりお茶を濁すための表現に匹敵する英語の表現が載っています。微妙ではっきりしない表現は、日本が独占しているわけではありません。西洋にも紅茶を濁す表現があります。

（4）バラエティーにトンだ表現

ビジネスの話題は非常に範囲の狭いものです。値段が上がったり、下がったり、安定したりといったようなことはありますが、人間のように不倫、自殺、人殺しなどはありません。ビジネスの話を彩らせようと思うならば、劇場的な同義語を使うしかないのです。例えば、＜株価がずいぶん上がった＞を＜株価が宇宙船のように飛びたった＞というように表現したほうが印象的です。日本では、understatement（ものを控えめに言うこと）が美徳として見られていますが、西洋ではサーカスの演技者にふさわしい大げさな表現が許されています。

（5）堅苦しさは相手にとっても苦しい

　外国人から見て、日本人の最も印象的なところは堅苦しい礼儀正しさです。外国人は皆、自信のカタマリ、内気と縁がないものだという先入観を持つ日本人には、我々西洋人が名刺交換やお辞儀、挨拶をどんなに怖がっているか想像もつかないだろうと思います。この本で学べるひとつのキーポイントは、フォーマルなビジネス英語とカジュアルなビジネス英語です。形式ばった日本人の皆さんが、気の効かないビジネス相手に安心感を与えることができるような、多彩でフレキシブルな英語を使えるようになったら嬉しく思います。とにかく、適応性が大切です。すべての状況に適する文章が、本書にはあります。全文を暗記したら、すべての状況に適応出来るようになること間違いなしです。

（6）甘い言葉と説得力で西洋人のビジネスマンを誘惑 マタハリのサラリーマン版

　日本人は皆「アイ・ラブ・ユー」という英語の表現を知っていますが、外国人のビジネス相手をどうやって興奮させ、どうやって刺激を与えるかはまだ理解していないようです。その場の状況にあった適切な言葉や表現をうまく使いこなせるようになると、外国人のビジネスマンを操ることが出来るようになります。

　以下、大まかに各章のキーポイントを説明します。

第1・2・3章
レトリックの技：舌の柔道

●ビジネス英語を使いこなす日本人は、サイズ重視のシュワちゃん系のボディビルダーより、ジャッキー・チェン型のアクロバット的な柔軟性を身につけるべき。手元にあるものを武器として使える想像力、オープン・マインドが必要。

第1章
●話題を導入したり、切り替えたりする時の決まり文句。自分の話を印象的にする。ボリュームを与える言葉の綿入れは、時間稼ぎにも有効！

第2章
●間接疑問文を通した控え目な、責任を拡散させるような提案の仕方。

●間接疑問文で、膨大な英語のボキャブラリーを持ち歩く必要性から脱却。

●直接話法を使って非常にインパクトのある文章をマスター。

第3章

●適切な言葉が出てこなくて困った<u>こと</u>、文章が乱れてしまう<u>ところ</u>、何かクギリを付けたいと思う<u>感じ</u>の時に適用できる、<言葉の関節>things,stuff, directionなど無意味に近い漠然とした単語を使いこなす。これらは流暢な英語の秘密兵器だ！

第4・5・6・7・8章

プレゼンテーションとその後のこと

第4章

●和製英語のビジネス用語は今や英語になった。西洋人もビジネス流行語に弱く、使いこなせる人の演説を聴くと感激するのです！

●日本人がもっている潜在的な英語語彙は数百語に及びます。それを生かすためのトレーニング！

第5章

●現実的な人は、外国語でプレゼンを行う時の、分かりやすい参考資料や話の展開の重要性を理解してる。この章は、（1）プレゼンのための明確なチャート、（2）プレゼンでの情報や意見のつなぎ方、について。

第6章

●上司やクライアントがいない時は、本音で話そう。営業戦士でも、はめをはずしたいときがある！オフィスの中の喜怒哀楽、サラリーマンにも感情があるんだ！

第7章

●変装した"NO"の様々な表現を見破るためのアンテナ磨き！

第8章

●弱音を吐くな！ダメだと言われても、２４時間ファイトする日本人のビジネスマンは、最後のプッシュに必要な英語のための、説得力に富んだ修辞学のトリックを身につけられる。新しい自分、<国際ビジネス界のチャーチル>を発見。

第9・10章

全知の賢人を目指す

第9章

●賢く、世の中を見抜く力とグローバル的な視野を持つ人間として見られたいと思う人は、この章で夢をかなえられる。この章を消化できれば、オフィスの哲学者としてデビュー。

第10章

●アメリカのニュース媒体が強いこと、日本人が謙遜していること、この2つの理由から、日本人の企業家のストーリーは世界であまり知られていない。しかし、最近まで貧しかった日本で成功し、世界市場を支配するまでになった大物が、貧困を極めていたという幼いころの話は、西洋にあまりない感動的なものである。頭が丸く、教養のある人として見られたければ、このような日本の企業家、日本の武将、日本のビジネス著者を初め、欧米の企業家達や著者まで知る必要がある。日本のサラリーマンにまつわる、幅広い意味での＜文化＞を面白く説明できるようになるために、邦人のヒーローや外国人のヒーローを知ることは、会話を彩らせるための必要不可欠なトリックである。一次元的なサラリーマンの典型から脱皮し、ピーター・ドラッカーの小型日本版になることも可能。

第11章

●どの国のビジネスマンでも、残業のしすぎで疲れきって、脳がマヒしてしまう時がある。そのような危機の時＜省エネ英語＞に切り替えないと、知的産業上の一番貴重な財産である「脳」をメルトダウンの危険にさらすことになる。英語用の自動操縦措置を紹介。

　本書には国際ビジネスマンとして活躍するためのツールが目一杯詰め込まれています。本書を十分に活用し、個性豊かで、創造力やユーモアに富んだ、国際派ビジネスマンを目指されることを期待します。

INTRODUCTION

Till now, books purporting to teach business Japanese have concentrated on greetings and etiquette, or on polysyllabic financial and economic terms. Such texts, while enabling *gaijin* business people to glean news from the *Nihon Keizai Shimbun* over breakfast and then to make a truly exquisite performance of their bowing, scraping and business-card exchanging, signally failed to prepare them for the nitty-gritty, down-and-dirty of the meeting or presentation itself. The reader was equipped with all the knowledge but none of the know-how, armed with the appropriate weapons but firing only blanks—a master of the formal and the highbrow, but utterly without the adaptability needed to persuade, to negotiate, to wheedle, and to browbeat.

Even with the allegedly inscrutable Japanese, however, the ultimate purpose of business is to do business. They have not become an economic superpower merely by a fetishistic insistence on ceremonial, nor by informed discussions on the global economy. Japan has become top nation precisely because business is so intimate and natural a part of everyday life.

Instant Business Japanese enables you to function as a fully versatile businessperson in a Japanese environment. It provides you with all the tools—from velvet glove to iron fist—necessary to carry out business in Japan. Memorize everything in the book and you will be a wholly convincing replicant. Memorize everything in the book, *then* adapt it to your own needs, and you'll be a highly valuable specialist. *Instant Business Japanese* can change you from a bewildered floater into a proactive adder of value!

How will we effect this transformation? Simple. We will teach you to go beyond any preconceptions or stereotype views of "salarymen" you may have and enable you to relate to them as human beings! *If you can make the human connection first, then you can certainly make money later.*

Salarymen have heretofore been depicted as very one-dimensional. In Van Wolferen's *Enigma of Japanese Power* they are presented as members of a "submissive middle-class" whose minds have been "remodeled" through "lengthy submersions in an ice-cold river clad only in a loincloth." They are further zombified, it seems, by a culture of pornographic newspapers, violent comic books, and mindless TV programs.

We disagree. If the native of Bali feels most alive when dancing in a frenzied trance, if the modern American gets his most powerful rush when engaged in litigation, or if the Scandinavian feels intoxicating *lebensfreude* only when his sauna-warmed posterior tingles from the mingled smarts of birch rod and crisp snow, then it is in the office that the modern Japanese is most himself and "burns with a hard, gem-like flame." For the "corporate warrior" what, after all, could be nobler than the battle itself?

Far from sharing the common view of salarymen as a crowd of browbeaten nonentities, we choose to regard them as *the most vivid contemporary manifestation of the Japanese spirit. Instant Business Japanese* will introduce you to eleven sides of the multi-faceted salaryman, covering the whole gamut from the *tatemae* (respectable appearance) to the *honne* (seething inner feelings).

OUTLINE OF THE BOOK

To run through our agenda:

- Chapters 1, 2, and 3 will teach you how to speak with the the fluency necessary for think-on-your-feet situations.

- Chapter 4 will teach you the business jargon that turns salarymen on.

- Chapter 5 will teach you how the art of making chart-based presentations that can go on persuading even after you've packed up and gone home.

- Chapter 6 will teach you how to speak with a Banker's Trust-like frankness about your clients.

- Chapter 7 provides ghost-buster goggles for spotting wraith-like "no's" so polite and circumlocutory that you wouldn't know they were "no's" at all.

- Chapter 8 teaches you how to speak <u>eloquently</u> and <u>forcefully</u> when discretion has ceased to be the better part of valor.

- Chapters 9 provides you with ready-made pearls of Japanese <u>conventional wisdom</u> to strew throughout your presentations.

- Chapter 10 will teach you how to allude to the salaryman's <u>role models and heroes</u>—warriors, entrepreneurs, and management gurus.

- Chapter 11 will teach you how speak with <u>macho roughness</u> and <u>imprecision</u>.

THE CHAPTER LAYOUT

The chapters—with a few minor exceptions—are arranged according to the following pattern.

(1) An <u>English Briefing</u> outlines the thrust of the chapter.

(2) The <u>Sample Sentences</u> then introduce the themes of the chapter in easily digestible sentence form. Each sentence is provided in Japanese, romanized Japanese, and English. The sentences are divided into thematic groups for maximum intelligibility and memorizability.

(3) The <u>Dialogues</u> go on to show the language introduced in the sample sentences being used in a real-life situation—the story of McVitie Consulting's reorganization of Suzuki Denki. Each dialogue (of which there is usually one, but sometimes two per chapter) is given in a romanized Japanese, a standard Japanese, and an idiomatic English version.

(4) <u>English notes</u> accompany the Japanese dialogues, and Japanese notes the English dialogues. These provide additional information on business language and business practices in Japan in a discursive and relaxed style. They fulfil the role of a *senpai*, an older, more experienced mentor who provides advice and encouragment to his or her juniors.

HOW TO READ THE BOOK

For those readers who wish to know everything about business Japanese I recommend reading the book from cover to cover. For those readers who wish only to prepare for a specific business situation, intensive study of the appropriate chapter should be adequate. Remember, however, that if you jump around you will miss out on the development of the story of Suzuki Denki! For the more casual reader *Instant Business Japanese* can be leafed through at random as an entertainment. The introductions, sentences, dialogues, and notes are all of intrinsic interest and religiously avoid traditional textbook triteness (*Mount Fuji is big, I like sushi* etc.).

I should like to encourage the reader to practice saying the sentences aloud and with maximum expression, since *how* you say something is just as important as *what* you say. If you choose to speak in buzzwords, sound excited. If you refuse a request, sound pained. If you choose to dispense conventional wisdom, sound immensely solemn. If you choose to bluff, sound sincere.

Female readers may be rightly indignant to find women playing a minor role in the story of Suzuki Denki. The subtitle of this book, however, is "real-life skills for real-life situations" and, like it or not, Japanese business is very much a man's world. While they may feel sorry for the lot of the Office Lady, they should remember that they themselves are not obliged to conform to the Japanese pattern of graceful servility, since they will be perceived first as foreigners, *then* as women. Clutch that straw!

Naoko Ito knows that this book could not have been written, or indeed even have evolved, without her. I should like also to express my thanks to my turbo-charged former teachers, Sakamoto Sensei at The Central Japanese Language School and Yoko Ueno at the Zeus Academy. An embarrassed grunt of gratitude also to my colleagues and clients for providing me—albeit unconsciously—with material for the book. My thanks, finally, to my editor for his sweet-and-sour mixture of constructive suggestions and prudent emasculations.

Giles Murray

ONE

•

INTRODUCTORY PHRASES
&
PLAUSIBLE PADDING

ボリュームのある文章を目指す

DON'T BE A JERK, BE A SMOOTHIE

When called upon to speak with persuasive fluency at a presentation or meeting, a major difficulty faced by students of business Japanese is how to allocate memory space appropriately. The over-loaded *gaijin*-brain is forced to accomodate three distinct pieces of data at the same time—the original English of what it wishes to say, the Japanese for the key vocabulary, and the Japanese phrase in which to set that vocabulary: In addition, some memory space must be left free for the sentence-assembly process. Eager to give a professional impression, many businessmen memorize masses of polysyllabic jargon, only to find that this has so clogged up their mental computer that they haven't enough brainpower left to construct a coherent sentence. This results in jerky, clunking phrases, guaranteed to negate the positive impression created by individual buzzwords.

Take heart! There is no reason that your Japanese should founder like this. Impressive vocabulary and a polished sentence-setting for it are not mutually exclusive! It is possible to memorize entire linking phrases just like single words. Business Japanese can be reduced to easy-to-assemble, snap-on components. Overcome your memory block with our building blocks!

GIVE YOUR IDEAS A LIFT! PULL YOURSELF TOGETHER!

In a business setting, excessive brevity is a dangerous thing. You know your product or service inside out, but the other side needs time to absorb the new information you're presenting. If you make your points too concisely and too telegraphically, there is a danger that your audience will fail to pick up on them. A little extra volume, a little hot air gives time for ideas to sink in. Our ready-made link-phrases provide a *Wonderbra*-like lift and thrust for your opinions, rounding them out, and putting them unignorably in your audience's face. A little padding can be a useful attention-getter.

SOPHISTICATION AND SMOKESCREENS

In addition to making your Japanese smoother and less obviously foreign, our ready-made phrases can also conveniently soften and obscure the outlines of your meaning. In a classroom context when practicing Japanese one question has one right answer. In a business context, however, there may be one question, but there are a multiplicity of situation-appropriate filters that can be applied to the answer. Are you talking up your company to inflate the prices you charge? Are you attempting to paint a failure as a "useful learning experience" to the press or to your superiors? Our ready-made phrases make your Japanese sophisticated in the good and bad senses of the word—fluent and fine-sounding , but also disingenuous, ambivalent, and slippery. Ultimately this chapter can teach you to say nothing, but to say it well. Politics, anyone?

There are seven categories in this section: We offer a variety of ways to **1. introduce a topic** (*in terms of, regarding etc.*), to **2. link ideas and present additional information** (*in addition to, along with, in the same way etc.*) to **3. express points of view** (*from our point of view, looked at from another angle etc.*), to **4. make comparisons** (*compared to, if we liken x to y etc.*), to **5. discuss trends** (*trend-wise etc.*), to **6. speak positively about the future** (*we're gonna do whatever it takes*) and finally to **7. be ambiguous and hard to pin down** (*according to how you look at it this news is either very good or very bad etc.*)

1. INTRODUCING A TOPIC
話題の導入

● リストラに付きましては雇用に絶対手を出す
つもりはありません。

Risutora [*restru*cture] **ni tsukimashite** wa, koyō ni
zettai te o dasu tsumori wa arimasen.

As regards the restructuring, we have absolutely no
intention of laying anyone off.

- コストの面において国内生産はなかなか大変だ。

Kosuto [cost] **no men ni oite** kokunaiseisan wa nakanaka taihen da.

In terms of cost, producing things in Japan is pretty crazy.

- この新しい計画に対して、うちのスタンスは 100%積極的である。

Kono atarashii keikaku **ni taishite**, uchi no sutansu [stance] wa hyaku paasento [percent] sekkyokuteki de aru.

Re the new plan, we're one-hundred percent behind it.

- PC分野において利益マージンが薄くなっても、 サーバーのほうはまだ潤いがのこっている。

PC bunya **ni oite** rieki maajin [margin] ga usuku natte mo, saabaa [server] no hō wa mada uruoi ga nokotte iru.

Even if margins **in the** PC business are wafer thin, there's still some money to be made in servers.

- 中国への進出に関して言えば、危険と可能性は 表裏一体である。

Chūgoku e no shinshutsu **ni kanshite ieba**, kiken to kanōsei wa hyōri ittai de aru.

As regards expansion into China, danger and opportunity are two sides of the same coin.

● ブランド性の点についてみますと日本の消費者は
　妙にうるさいと言えます。

Burando [brand]-sei no ten **ni tsuite mimasu to**, Nihon no
shōhisha wa myō-ni urusai to iemasu.

If we look at brands, Japanese consumers are
unusually demanding.

● 競合相手のやり方をみてみると、やっぱりうちと違う。

Kyōgō-aite no yarikata **o mite miru to**, yappari
uchi to chigau.

When you have a look at our competitors' way of working, it's
quite obvious they're doing things differently from us.

● ソフトと言えば何といってもアメリカの西海岸ですね。

Sofuto [soft] **to ieba** nan to itte mo Amerika no
Nishikaigan desu ne.

When it comes to software the West Coast's
where it's all happening!

● 外国人の記者に説明するにあたって、広報部の
　バナナが担当者です。

Gaikokujin no kisha ni setsumei suru **ni atatte**,
kōhōbu no Banana ga tantōsha desu.

For briefings to foreign journalists, Mr. Banana
of the PR section is in charge.

● この会社をめぐる噂はすべてウソだ。我々は
総会屋に一銭も払っていない。

Kono kaisha **o meguru** uwasa wa subete uso da.
Wareware wa sōkaiya ni issen mo haratte inai.

All the rumors **concerning** this firm are lies. We have never
paid a single penny to any extortionist!

2. LINKING IDEAS & ADDING INFORMATION
アイデアを結び付ける／情報を付け加える

● AVの他に、その会社はホワイトグッズを作っている。

AV **no hoka ni**, sono kaisha wa howaito-guzzu
[white goods] o tsukutte iru.

In addition to audiovisual equipment, that firm
also produces white goods.

● 会社の成長と規模拡大につれ、問題の規模も
変わってくる。

Kaisha no seichō to kibokakudai **ni tsure**, mondai
no kibo **mo** kawatte kuru.

As a company gets bigger, its problems get bigger **too.**

● 利益だけではなく、人材、つまり人間性を考え
あわせなくてはいけない。

Rieki **dake de wa naku**, jinzai, tsumari ningensei o
kangae-**awasenakute** wa ikenai.

Thinking purely about profits **isn't enough**, you've got to
think of the employees—the human side of things—**too**.

● ヒット商品作りを目指すときは、質と共に
デザインの要素も必要です。

Hitto [hit] shōhinzukuri o mezasu toki wa, shitsu **to tomo ni**
dezain [design] no yōso mo hitsuyō desu.

When trying to create a hit product, **in addition to** quality,
design is a key element.

● 日本の市場は、他の先進国と同様に成熟してきました。

Nihon no shijō wa, hoka no senshinkoku **to dōyō ni**
seijuku shite kimashita.

Just like other developed countries, the Japanese
market has now reached maturity.

● 円高を背景に輸出量が伸びたのは珍しいことに見える。

Endaka **o haikei ni** yushutsuryō ga nobita no wa
mezurashii koto ni mieru.

Against a background of a strong yen, the fact that exports
increased is pretty amazing.

● パチンコを除くと、日本経済のすべての業界は
　　かなり苦しんでいます。

Pachinko **o nozoku to**, Nihon-keizai no subete no
gyōkai wa kanari kurushinde imasu.

With the single exception of Pachinko, every area of the
Japanese economy is hurting *bad*.

● 困ったことに部長がマーケティング戦略を立てた。
　　我々はそれに基づいて行動しなければならない。

Komatta koto ni buchō ga maaketingu [marketing]
senryaku o tateta. Wareware wa **sore ni motozuite**
kōdō shinakereba naranai.

Unfortunately the department chief made this
marketing plan, and we have to act **according to it**.

● 会社の売り上げ高がこのまま伸びていくと、そろそろ
　　大手と言っていいほどの規模になる。

Kaisha no uriagedaka ga **kono mama nobite iku to**,
sorosoro oote to itte ii hodo no kibo ni naru.

If the firm's sales continue growing **like this**, soon we'll
be big enough to be called "blue chip."

- 日本では、コングロマリット型の組織が多い。**具体的な例でいえば**、百貨店、電車、バスから映画館、不動産までの業界で活躍している東急があります。

Nihon de wa, konguromaritto [conglomerate]-gata no soshiki ga ooi. **Gutaiteki-na rei de ieba**, hyakkaten, densha, basu [bus] kara eigakan, fudōsan made no gyōkai de katsuyaku shite iru Tōkyū ga arimasu.

In Japan there are many conglomerates-type companies. **To give one example**, take Tōkyū which runs businesses ranging from department stores, trains and buses to movie theaters and real estate.

3. POINTS OF VIEW & WAYS OF PUTTING IT
見方 & 言い方

- 我々にとって、その会社の破産はいいことだ。

Wareware ni totte, sono kaisha no hasan wa ii koto da.

From our perspective, the bankruptcy of that company is a good thing.

- 視点を変えてみると、解雇されることはチャンスだよ。

Shiten o kaete miru to, kaiko sareru koto wa chansu [chance] da yo.

If you look at it another way, being fired could be a great opportunity!

● 新しい技術は成功の鍵を握っている。**言い換えれば、**
うちも何か色気のある製品を作らないとそろそろ
ダメということです。

Atarashii gijutsu wa seikō no kagi o nigitte iru.
Iikaereba, uchi mo nani ka iroke no aru seihin o
tsukuranai to sorosoro dame to iu koto desu.

It's new technology that's the key to success. **To put it
differently**, if we don't make some sexy products
soon, we're history.

4. COMPARISONS
比較 & 例え

● バブルがはじける前に比べて、現在の売上高は
すずめの涙にすぎない。

Baburu [bubble] ga hajikeru mae **ni kurabete,**
genzai no uriagedaka wa suzume no namida ni suginai.

In comparison to the old days of the bubble economy, our present sales are absolutely pitiful (*lit: no more than a sparrow's tears*).

● 会社を動物に例えれば、うちはゴジラではなくて、
愛玩犬みたいなもんです。

Kaisha o dōbutsu **ni tatoereba,** uchi wa Gojira [Godzilla]
de wa nakute, aiganken mitai na mon desu.

If we liken our firm to an animal, it's more
of a lap-dog than a Godzilla!

5. TRENDS & OPINION
傾向 & 意見

● 流れとしてやはりこれからは独立型PCではなく、
イントラネットの時代になっていきます。

Nagare toshite yahari korekara wa dokuritsugata PC de wa
naku, intoranetto [intranet] no jidai ni natte ikimasu.

> **The trend is**, of course, shifting from stand-alone
> PC's to the Intranet.

● 傾向として日本経済の空洞化は認めざるを得ない。

> **Keikō toshite** Nihon keizai no kūdōka wa
> mitomezaru o enai.

> The hollowing-out of the Japanese economy is
> an undeniable and inevitable **trend**.

● サラリーマンは創造性に乏しいと言う声が最近
聞こえてきます。

Sarariiman [salaryman] wa sōzōsei ni toboshii to iu
koe ga saikin **kikoete kimasu**.

> Recently **the view** that Japanese businessmen lack
> creativity **has been gaining ground**.

6. BEING POSITIVE ABOUT THE FUTURE
前向きの表現

● いろいろな意味で社員の仕事に対しての
考え方を変えたい。

Iroiro-na imi de shain no shigoto ni taishite no
kangaekata o kaetai.

On a variety of levels I want to change the way our
employees think about their work.

● 新しいパソコン通信時代に向かって、模索して
いる。その糸口として、アメリカでの
市場の動きを見極めたい。

Atarashii pasokon [personal computer] tsūshinjidai ni
mukatte, mosaku shite iru. **Sono itoguchi toshite**,
Amerika de no shijō no ugoki o mi-kiwametai.

We're feeling our way forward toward the age of PC communications. **To give us some ideas**, we're looking
very closely at the American market.

● この業界の最先端に立ちたいという夢を持っています。
そこへ到達するためには、なんでもやるよ。

Kono gyōkai no saisentan ni tachitai to iu yume o motte
imasu. **Soko e tōtatsu suru tame ni wa**,
nan demo yaru yo.

We've got a dream of being the leaders in this field, and we'll
do whatever is necessary **to get there**.

● これから目指すべきことは流通のコストダウン、
それからブランド性の強化。この両方を達成
できれば、何とか先が見えてくる。

Korekara mezasu-beki koto wa ryūtsū no kosutodaun
[costdown,] sorekara burando [brand]-sei no kyōka. **Kono
ryōhō o tassei dekireba**, nan to ka saki ga miete kuru.

From now on we've got to aim to cut distribution costs, and
reinforce our brands. **If we can do these two things**, then we
have some idea where we're going.

7. BEING AMBIVALENT
曖昧な表現／煙幕をはる

● うちの会社の人はどちらかというと保守的です。

Uchi no kaisha no hito wa **dochira ka to iu to** hoshuteki desu.

Our employees are, **I suppose**, a little on the conservative side.

● このニュースは見方によっていいか悪いか意見が別れる。

Kono nyūsu [news] wa **mikata ni yotte** ii ka warui ka
iken ga wakareru.

According to how you look at it, this news can
be interpreted as either good or bad.

● 計算の方法によって違うが、いずれにしても、今年の
業績はよくないであろう。

Keisan no hōhō ni yotte chigau ga, **izure ni shite mo**,
kotoshi no gyōseki wa yokunai de arō.

Things vary according to how you calculate it, but, **whichever
way you look at it**, this year's results are hardly good.

● マルチメディアに対する政策は、今のところまだ未定です。

Maruchimedia [multimedia] ni taisuru seisaku wa,
ima no tokoro mada mitei desu.

At the present time we have **not yet** developed
a multimedia strategy.

● 利益という視点からみると有望でなくても、
会社の雰囲気は生き生きとしています。

Rieki to iu shiten kara miru to yūbō denakute mo,
kaisha no fun'iki wa ikiiki to shite imasu.

If you just look at profit things look grim, but the
atmosphere in the firm is highly dynamic.

● このプロジェクトが失敗したのはいくつかの理由による。

Kono purojekuto [project] ga shippai shita no wa
ikutsu ka no riyū ni yoru.

There are any number of reasons why this project failed.

● 正直にいうとその分野から撤退したいと思っています。

Shōjiki-ni iu to sono bunya kara tettai shitai to omotte imasu.

To be honest, we're thinking of withdrawing
from that field entirely.

1

Briefing:
Nani ga warui?

Chuck: Hajimemashite, Chuck to mōshimasu. Yoroshiku o-negai shimasu.

Suzuki: Suzuki to mōshimasu. Yoroshiku. Dōzo, suwatte kudasai. Kyō no uchiawase no mokuteki wa nan desu ka?

Chuck: Maa, kyō wa, mazu, onsha ga kakaete iru mondai ni tsuite ikutsu ka o-kiki shitai to omotte orimasu. Uchiawase to iimasu ka, Buriifingu [Briefing] to iu koto nan desu ga.

Suzuki: Yoshi. Fuku-shachō no Tomita ga chōki-senryaku no tantō no mono desu kara, kare ga shitsumon ni o-kotae shimasu.

Chuck: **Donna kakudo kara mite mo**, onsha wa ii jōkyō ni aru to wa iemasen. **Saiseiki ni kurabete**, uriagedaka wa hanbun made ochite imasu. Sore o oomaka de mo ii desu kara setsumei shite moraemasu ka?

Tomita: Baburu [bubble] ga hajikete kara, Nihon-keizai zentai ga teimei suru naka de, wareware **to onaji yō ni** akaji o dashite iru kaisha wa sukunakunai desu yo. **Sore ni**, Amerika no gijutsuteki-na kaifuku toka, Nihon no ōgon jidai ga owatta **to iu koe mo kikaremasu.**

Chuck: Ee, ee. Mō chotto gutaiteki-na riyū o teiji shite moraemasu deshō ka?

Tomita: Maa, kaisha no uriage no gekigen **ni kan shite ieba**, ikutsuka no riyū, ikutsu ka no bimyō-na gen'in ga arimasu ne.

Chuck: Gijutsu **to iu shiten kara mite miru to**, dō desu ka?

Tomita: Maa, gijutsu **o meguru** mondai desu to, gyōkai-nai no kaihatsu no peesu [pace] ga hijō ni hayaku narimashite... **Ichigai ni iu no wa nakanaka muzukashii. Nagare toshite** yahari Waapuro [*word-proc*essor] kara pasokon [*perso*nal *com*puter] e no ikō ga sukoshi medachi-hajimeta. **Sore ni tomonatte**, konpyūta [computer]-gyōkai no keikō ga tanoshisa, tsukai-yasusa, tsumari Amerika-jin no hippii [hippy] rakudaisei no konomi no mono ni henbō shimashite...

Watanabe: Maa, tanoshii to iu koto wa tashika-ni kiipointo [keypoint] deshō.

Suzuki: Naraba kongo, tanoshisa to iu hassō **o chūshin ni oita** kaisha-zukuri o kentō shitai. **Sore o suru ni atatte**, Tomita-kun, kimi wa ashita kara Tshatsu [T-shirt] ni jiinzu [jeans] de shussha shinasai!

ブリーフィング：何が悪い？

Chuck and Watanabe have their first meeting with the founder and CEO of Suzuki Denki, Suzuki, and his right-hand man, Tomita. They attempt to elicit information about the problems, both marketing and technical, that the company is facing, but Tomita, who feels he is in for a rough ride, is stalling and being evasive. In the end, however, he gets his comeuppance.

チャック： 始めまして、チャックと申します。よろしくお願いします。

スズキ： 鈴木と申します。よろしく。どうぞ、すわってください。今日の打ち合わせの目的は何ですか？

チャック： まあ、今日は、まず、御社が抱えている問題についていくつかお聞きしたいと思っております。打ち合わせといいますか、ブリーフィングということなんですが。

スズキ： よし。副社長の富田が長期戦略の担当の者ですから、彼が質問にお答えします。

チャック： どんな角度から見ても、御社はいい状況にあるとは言えません。最盛期に比べて、売上高は半分まで落ちています。それを大まかでもいいですから説明してもらえますか。

トミタ： バブルがはじけてから、日本経済全体が低迷する中で、我々と同じように赤字を出している会社は少なくないですよ。それに、アメリカの技術的な回復とか、日本の黄金時代が終わったという声もきかれます。

チャック： ええ、ええ。もうちょっと具体的な理由を提示してもらえますでしょうか？

Project Briefing: What's wrong?

チャックさんと渡部さんは、鈴木電気を訪れ創設者である鈴木社長と富田副社長に面会しています。彼等は長期戦略担当の富田副社長に会社が直面している問題についての説明を求めますが、期待するような具体的な回答が返ってきません。

Chuck: How do you do, I'm Chuck Bones.

Suzuki: How do you, I'm Shunichi Suzuki. Please, have a seat. So…what's the aim of today's meeting.

Chuck: Well, today, to start with we want to ask you some questions about the problems you've got. Basically you brief us…

Suzuki: Right. Since Mr. Tomita here is in charge of our long-term strategy, he'll answer any questions you have.

Chuck: Fine. Well, **whichever way you look at it**, your firm's not in a good way. **Compared to their peak**, your sales have fallen by fifty percent. Can you explain that—even very roughly is fine.

Tomita: Well, since the end of what we call the bubble economy, the Japanese economy as a whole has been pretty stagnant. **In these conditions** the number of firms who, like us, have moved into loss is by no means small. **In addition**, there's the technological revival in the United States, why, some people are even saying the Golden Age of Japan is over…

Chuck: Yes, yes. But can't you give us some more detailed explanations.

トミタ： まあ、会社の売り上げの激減に関して言えば、いくつかの理由、いくつかの微妙な原因がありますね。

チャック： 技術という視点から見てみると、どうですか。

トミタ： まあ、技術をめぐる問題ですと、業界内の開発のペースが非常に早くなりまして、一概に言うのはなかなか難しい。流れとしてやはりワープロからパソコンへの移行が少し目立ち始めた。それに伴って、コンピュータ業界の傾向が楽しさ、使いやすさ一つまりアメリカ人のヒッピー落第生の好みのものに変貌しまして…

ワタナベ： まあ、楽しいということは確かにキーポイントでしょう。

スズキ： ならば今後、楽しさと言う発想を中心に置いた会社づくりを検討したい。それをするにあたって、富田君、きみは明日からT-シャツにジーンズで出社しなさい。

Tomita: Well, **as regards** our decline in sales, there are numerous reasons, numerous subtle causes...

Chuck: What about from a technological point of view?

Tomita: Well, **as for** problems **concerning** technology, the pace of development has speeded up astonishingly. **It's rather difficult to generalize**. Recently **the trend** to switch from word-processors to PC's has become very marked. **Furthermore**, the emphasis in the computer world is on *fun* and *user-friendliness*. In short everything's changing along the lines of hippy college dropout philosophy...

Watanabe: Yes the element of enjoyment is certainly crucial...

Suzuki: Well, if that is the case then, I want to look closely at this idea of creating a company **based on** the fun concept. **As a start**, Mr. Tomita, from tomorrow you will come to work in jeans and a T-shirt!

Know-it-all Notes

• Yoroshiku onegai shimasu   よろしくお願いします

The Japanese cudgel their brains wondering how to translate this phrase into English. However, meaning something like "I beseech your favor" it is, along with its accompanying bow, without English equivalent. Use it as polite phrase to mumble when handing over your **meishi** (business card) or at the end of a phonecall or a presentation. Business decisions might be made not according to the worth of your firm's product or service, but according to your **taido** (attitude). If you've diligently pitched someone for two or three years showing appropriate humility, it may be felt that your request for favor deserves to be rewarded with an order!

• Uchiawase   打ち合わせ

There are other words for meeting—the katakana *meeting* or *briefing* (both a little informal, and the latter very advertising-speak), or the Japanese **kaigi** (rather formal, suggesting the participation of a large number of people, and perhaps even the reaching of a decision).

• Onsha   御社

Though this should not be translated into a Charlie Chan-ish *Your honorable company*, the sentiment implied is certainly respectful. Alternatives would be **kisha**, or **Suzuki Denki-san**.

• Bubble ga hajikete kara   バブルがはじけてから

Since the bubble burst. This is the "bubble economy," the name given to Japan's economic boom in the 1980s. The "bubble" was fueled by cheap credit, a frenziedly rising stock market, and sky-rocketing land prices. The Nikkei index rose to 38,912, and it was calculated that the grounds of the Imperial Palace in Tokyo were worth more than all the land in Canada. This was the period when the Japanese took their noses off the grindstone for the first time after the war, and, just as Lord Byron "awoke and found himself famous," they awoke and noticed they were rich!

For readers interested in learning more about this period Christopher Wood's *The Bubble Economy* and *The End of Japan, Inc.* can be recommended.

A useful related phrase is Bubble-no-kōishō—*post-bubble syndrome*, or *fall-out*.

• Kaifuku　回復

Tomita is here referring not so much to the bouncing back of the Big Three automakers (characterized by GM's Saturn, "a Japanese car made in America") as to the extraordinary growth of relatively young high-tech firms such as Microsoft, Sun Microsystems, and Compaq. In the early 1990s the only American firms to advertise on Japanese TV were relatively low-tech fast-food chains or beverage makers. Now Ford, Chrysler, Hewlett-Packard, and Compaq all have large-scale TV advertising with Sun even sponsoring the major evening business news program, "World Business Satellite."

• Gekigen　激減

Sudden, dramatic shrinking. The prefix geki is very common. Consider gekiyasu (ultra-cheap), and for curries, gekikara (ultra-hot.)

• Hippy rakudaisei　ヒッピー落第生

As far as Tomita is concerned good businessmen graduate from university, have well-cropped hair, and wear gray suits. Anyone who leaves university early, as for example Bill Gates who dropped out of Harvard, is—however successful they might be—no more than a *Hippy dropout.*

• T-shirts　Tシャツ

Hoping to *californicate* the salaryman mind and stimulate business in men's fashion at the same time, many firms have introduced a Casual Friday into their working week. Employees are encouraged and often forced to wear casual and colorful clothing to the office on this day, and develop dynamic and creative personalities to match their newly-purchased check pants and silk cravats.

物知り英語ノート

• How do you do?

日本語で挨拶するときに必ず「よろしくお願いします」と言いますが、このような最初から自分を低くした表現は西洋ではありえないので英語に直訳することはできません。ですから無理に言葉で表現する必要はありません。

• I'm Chuck Bones

英語で自己紹介する時には必ずフルネームで自分の名前を相手に告げて下さい。**I'm Suzuki** のように自分を名字だけで紹介すると非常に個性の無い人として見られがちです。**I'm Ken Suzuki, please call me Ken.** のように自己紹介するほうが相手も名前を覚えやすく親切といえます。どうしても避けて欲しい日本人のよくする間違いは、**Mr. Chuck** のようにファーストネームに **Mr.** をつけることです。植民地の人が西洋人に迎合するとき使うような英語になってしまいます。

• Please, have a seat

"おすわり下さい" **Please <u>do</u> sit down／Please, <u>take</u> a seat** も使うことができます。

• Well

この言葉は実際、無意味に近いものですが、日本語の「まあ」や「まず」のように会話のテーマを変える時のサインのようなものになっています。会話に柔らかさそして潤いを与える役割をしています。

• Basically

"つまり" ビジネスの話をかいつまんで話す時に使われる副詞です。

• Right

日本人が使う「はい」という意味の全てをYesでは表現できません。ここでは「わかった」「あなたの言うことは理解した」という意味ですので、**Right** を使っています。同じように **Fine** も使えます。

• In charge of

"の担当" **responsible for** も同じように使われます。

• Whichever way you look at it

"どうみても"間接的な言い方をすることで相手のショックを和らげることができます。

• Not in a good way

これはずばり "bad" と言うよりも軟らかい言い方です。このようなデリケートな言い方は Diplomatic、Tactful (思いやりのある) といいます。

• What we call the bubble economy

バブルのような和製英語を使う時、英語の表現にあるものかどうかを確認しない限り、"いわゆる"という意味の言葉を念のため付け加えた方が誤解を生む確率が低くなります。

• Stagnant

もともとは池の水が淀んで腐っていることを意味しますが、経済用語として "不活発な"、"停滞" 等に使用されます。

• In addition

"それに"何かを言い足したい時に使われますが、Andより響きのよい迫力のある表現です。

• Golden Age of Japan is over

富田さんはピーター・タスカの『日本の時代は終わったか?』という著書のタイトルを借用したと思われます。

• Yes, yes

相手の話にイライラした時、会話のペースを早くしたい時に使われます。日本語で「はい、はい、はい」と連続して言う時も同じようような状況に陥っているときでしょう。

• As regards

"に関して" regarding と同じように使えます。

• Numerous subtle causes

"いくつかの微妙な原因" 富田さんはここで月並なことを言いまくり、会社が抱えている問題から皆の注意をそらそうとしています。このような行為を Throwing out smokescreens／Blow smoke up my ass (煙幕をはる) と言います。同じような意味で使われる Bullshitting は、

うさん臭いことを並べ、ごまかそうとするがその行為が相手に見破られているときに使われます。このような行為をする人を He is a bull-shitter. と言うことができます。

• As for problems concerning technology

英語の表現として必要以上に長い言い方で、このような気取った言い方を pompous（もったいぶった）と言います。一般的には As for technological problems と言えるのですが、富田さんは話しの核心に近づきたくないため、ここでも煙幕を張っています。

• Hippy college dropouts

富田さんは創造性に乏しい団塊世代の代表的人物で、内面より外見で人を評価しています。彼のような人にとって、スーツを着た髪の毛の短い、全く才能のない人は、長髪の型にはまらない天才より価値のある存在です。彼自身は保守的（Conventional）で慣習に逆らうことができないのです。

• Jeans and a T-shirt

鈴木電気の鈴木社長は Silicon Valley のカジュアルなコーポレートカルチャーを導入することで、会社を活気づかせようとしています。このような傾向は最近多くの会社で見られ、「カジュアルデイ」もそのひとつといえます。

TWO

•

INDIRECT QUESTIONS & DIRECT SPEECH COAXING AND WHEEDLING

あなたはストレートですか？

NOUN-DEPENDENCE CLINIC

One of the key points that the student of Japanese *must* understand is that speaking fluently and naturally depends far less on knowing the precise word appropriate to a certain situation than on the ability to manipulate a small number of basic words to fit any situation whatsoever.

Consider the following example. A foreign student of English, eager to deploy hard-memorized nouns and reluctant to risk a long sentence might say **"I do not know the situation of the company" (9 words)**. A native speaker, however, substituting a more dynamic indirect question for the static and abrupt noun **"situation"** would say something like **"I don't know whether that company's doing well or not" (13 words)**. *Native speakers instinctively prefer longer verb phrases composed of simple elements to single, lifeless nouns.*

Failing to locate the appropriate noun in the warehouse of his dictionary, the arthritic-brained language learner is reduced to impotent silence. By contrast, the skilled and pragmatic linguist uses any available part of speech to rig up a substitute-phrase. Indulging our fondness for metaphor, we might call this inventory-reducing, productivity-enhancing technique, the *just-in-time method of speaking*. This chapter aims to maximize the productivity of your basic vocabulary by enhancing its flexibility. We will show you how to reduce your exposure to easy-to-forget nouns by spreading your risk through investing in indirect and direct speech!

ON WITH THE KID-GLOVES !

The tendency to end a sentence with **ne** (*isn't that so?*, or *don't you think so too?*) is a classic indicator of the consensuality that characterizes Japanese society. Indeed, anyone who has listened to the endless stream of "**eeh's**" and "**hai's**" (*Oh, indeed, yes, I hear what you say*) which punctuate telephone calls knows that the Japanese like to encourage one another in conversation, feeding their interlocutor the next line like a good-natured prompter. The role of the indirect question is similar. Rather than state your opinion aggressively in anticipation of resistance, you advance your opinion cautiously, tenderly wooing the support of your audience. The indirect question is best considered as yet another "spoonful of sugar that helps the consensus-medicine go down."

EUROPEAN SENSIBILITY

You will see from the example sentences just how oblique and indirect an indirect question can get: Notice that if **de wa nai ka** (*is it not*) is too straight, you can dilute it to **to itte ii no de wa nai deshō ka** (*might it not be possible to say that*). Further, if **omou** (*think*) is too confident, substitute a more nebulous **kan-**

jimasu (*feel*) or a yō na ki ga shimasu (*feel somewhat that*). In short, the indirect question's most significant role is to introduce a reverse gung-ho element to a discussion. It is equivalent to the (rather British?) English—*might it not be better to, may it not be wiser to, surely it would be more prudent to* etc.

1. EASY INDIRECT QUESTIONS
簡単な間接疑問文

● マルチメディアはどんなかたちで展開していくか、
　それはまだ誰もわからない。

Maruchimedia [multimedia] wa **donna katachi de** tenkai shite iku **ka**, sore wa mada dare mo wakaranai.

No one really knows yet quite **in what way** multimedia is going to develop.

● あのオヤジはどこまでインターネットの意義を理解
　しているのか心配だよ。

Ano oyaji wa **doko made** Intaanetto [Internet] no igi o rikai shite iru no ka shinpai da yo.

I'm a bit worried about **how far** that old geezer really understands the significance of the Internet.

● 我々の強みは、やはりデザインなんだ。それを
デジタル時代に応じた形でどう生かせるかが
これからの課題だ。

Wareware no tsuyomi wa, yahari dezain [design]
nan' da. Sore o dejitaru [digital]-jidai ni ōjita katachi
de **dō** ikaseru **ka** ga korekara no kadai da.

Our strongpoint is design, and the big question now is **how**
can we exploit that in a form appropriate to the digital age.

● 日本人のビジネスマンは、毎日遅くまでいったい何を
やっているのか非常に不思議なところだ。

Nihonjin no bijinesuman [businessman] wa, mainichi
osoku made **ittai nani** o yatte iru no **ka** hijō ni
fushigi-na tokoro da.

It really is very mysterious **just what** Japanese businessmen
are doing until so late everyday.

2. COMPLEX INDIRECT QUESTIONS
複雑な間接疑問文

● 中国にコミットするかどうか、それはまだ検討中である。

Chūgoku ni komitto [commit] suru **ka dō ka**, sore wa
mada kentōchū de aru.

We haven't yet decided **whether or not** to commit
ourselves to the Chinese market.

engage in

● 会社の再編成を行うか、つぶれるか、
　どちらかしかない。

Kaisha no saihensei o okonau **ka**, tsubureru **ka**.
dochira ka shika nai.

Ultimately **we have a simple choice between** restructuring
or going under.

● 我々はほかの会社とどう違うか、我々の特徴は何で
　あるかを再定義したい。

Wareware wa hoka no kaisha to **dō** chigau **ka**, wareware
no tokuchō wa **nan** de aru **ka** o saiteigi shitai.

I want to redefine exactly **how** we differ from our rivals, exactly
what our unique points are.

● こちらが確認したいのは、このプロジェクトはいつ
　どんなかたちで現実化するかということだ。

Kochira ga kakunin shitai no wa, kono purojekuto [project] wa
itsu donna katachi de genjitsuka suru ka to iu koto da.

On our side what we want to make sure of is **when and in
what form** this project is going to be carried out.

3. INDIRECT QUESTIONS—What should we do?

するべきこと

● 今日は、これからの家電メーカーはどうあるべきか
について話したい。

Kyō wa, korekara no kaden meekaa [maker] wa **dō
aru beki ka** ni tsuite hanashitai.

Today I want to talk about **how** electronics firms will
have to evolve in the future.

● 問題になっているのは、日本の成長期が終わってから
サラリーマンはどう変わるべきかだ。

Mondai ni natte iru no wa, Nihon no seichōki ga owatte
kara sarariiman [salaryman] wa **dō kawaru beki ka** da.

The big question is, given that Japan's days of heady growth
are over, **how** should the Japanese *salaryman* adapt?

● 直面しなくてはいけないのは、通貨の変動にどう
取り組むべきかでしょう。

Chokumen shinakute wa ikenai no wa, tsūka no hendō
ni **dō tori-kumu beki ka** deshō.

How to cope with currency fluctuations is one problem
we have to work out.

4. QUESTION FORM FOR HUMBLE & DIFFIDENT SUGGESTIONS
疑問型の謙遜じみた提案

● 日本は、19世紀の英国と同じように、世界の
工場と呼んでいいのではないか。

Nihon wa, jūkyū-seiki no eikoku to onaji yō ni, sekai no
kōjō to **yonde ii no de wa nai ka**.

Could one not say that Japan is now, like England in the nineteenth century, "the workshop of the world?"

● この市場の動きをどう読めばいいのか、それを
検討したい。

Kono shijō no ugoki o **dō yomeba ii no ka**, sore o kentō shitai.

What we want to check up on is **how** we **should** interpret
these market movements.

● あいつを早めに子会社に移した方がいいのでは
ないかと思う。

Aitsu o hayame ni kogaisha ni utsushita hō ga ii
no **de wa nai ka to omou**.

My feeling is that it might be better for that guy to be
moved to some insignificant subsidiary *asap.*

● マルチメディアって皆騒いでいるけど、実際にそれが
　何であるかまだ誰にも解らない、と言って
　いいんじゃないかと感じます。

Maruchimedia [multimedia] 'tte mina sawaide iru kedo,
jissai ni sore ga **nan** de aru **ka** mada dare ni mo
wakaranai **to itte iin' ja nai ka to kanjimasu**.

My feeling is that everyone's getting hysterical about
multimedia, but, in fact, **it's reasonable** to say that no
one really knows what multimedia is!

● この部には、一番無能な人間が集中しているのでは
　ないかと思った。

Kono bu ni wa, ichiban munō-na ningen ga shūchū
shite iru no **de wa nai ka to omotta**.

I got the feeling that perhaps they'd put all the most
useless people in that one division.

● 技術者じゃない人も、一人ぐらい役員にすれば
　いいのではないかと思う。

Gijutsusha ja nai hito mo, hitori gurai yakuin ni sureba
ii no de wa nai ka to omou.

I think it might not be a bad idea to have at least one
director who isn't an engineer.

5. THE HANGING "TO"

＜と＞中でおわる文書

PREGNANT PAUSES

Whereas the first four sections of this chapter deal with indirect questions, the fifth deals with the most indirect form of speech there is—*silence*. The silence is introduced by the hanging "to" equivalent to "if."

This usage, which we have dubbed "**The hanging to as a discreet threat**" is equivalent to **ALARMIST REMARK + UNEASY SILENCE** in English. "*If you don't rethink your product line…*" (Implied: "*you're going to go bankrupt*"). Of course, in Japanese it would be excessively indelicate to spell out the dire consequences, thus the "to" is left to hang, rich in gloomy implication. It is a handy form for a foreigner to know, as a great effect can be achieved with only half a sentence.

Since what is left to be inferred is often more significant than what is actually said, the tone in which small and intrinsically meaningless words (to ka, to, sore de) are left to echo and fade can be the clearest indicator of whether things are going well for you or not! It is very important to learn to distinguish between positively and negatively charged silences!

● ネーミングを重視しないと…

Neemingu [naming] o jūshi shinai **to**…

I want to emphasize that you must take product-naming seriously, or else… (*something terrible will happen*)

● リストラを行わないと…

Risutora [*restructure*]o okonowanai **to**…

If you don't undertake a restructuring then…
(*something terrible will happen*)

6. DRAMA THROUGH DIRECT SPEECH
劇場的な直接話法

DEADHEADS NEED NO VERBS

The final section introduces **Drama Through Direct Speech**. Just as the deadhead or beachbum has dispensed altogether with bothersome verbs of thinking or saying and gives his opinions thus: *And I was like "wow! that's real cool" and she was like "yeah! go for it!,"* the same verb-and-reported-speech-free-zone exists in the Japanese language for the grammatically-challenged salaryman. It is extremely vivid and thus particularly popular with ad-men and salesmen eager to infect clients with their enthusiasm: *And I guarantee that every teenager from Tokyo to Timbuktoo will be like "I've gotta have one of those or my life ain't worth living."* At the same time both very simple to master and highly idiomatic it is a useful form for the foreigner to know.

● 「車はRVじゃないとね」という考え方が
　　　若者の間で一般化した。

"Kuruma wa RV ja nai to ne" to iu kangaekata ga wakamono no aida de ippanka shita.

Among young people the notion that **"if you have a car at all it's got to be an off-road vehicle"** is pretty general now.

● 「皆ルイ・ヴィトンだから、あたしも」という
　　　動機も強い。

"Mina Louis Vuitton da kara, atashi mo" to iu dōki mo tsuyoi.

Among reasons-to-buy **"Everyone else has got a Vuitton bag, so I'd better get one too"** is very powerful.

● 腹をくくって「これからたたかいが始まるぞ」と
　　思いました。

Hara o kukutte **"korekara tatakai ga hajimaru zo"** to
omoimashita.

I felt something like **"I'm ready, and now the fight's really
going to start."**

● 最近の消費者は「コンドームを買うなら、蛍光じゃない
　　とつまらない」と思っているようだ。

Saikin no shōhisha wa **"Condom o kau nara, keikō ja nai
to tsumanai"** to omotte iru yō da.

Recently consumers seem to think **"If I buy condoms, they've
got to be glow-in-the-dark ones or I'm just not interested."**

● アメリカ的に「株価にマイナス影響を与えること
　　ならやめておこう」というのは、長期的に
　　　　考えるとよくない。

Amerika-teki-ni **"Kabuka ni mainasu [minus] eikyō o ataeru
koto nara yamete okō"** to iu no wa, chōkitekini
kangaeru to yokunai.

When you think about the American philosophy **"If it's bad
for the share price, don't even think about it,"** well,
obviously, it's no good over the long term.

2 | Genba no iken

Watanabe: Mada hayai dankai desu ga, iroiro-na chōsa o shite, shain to hanashite, nan toka kaisha no kanshoku o yomi-toreta to ieru to omoimasu.

Chuck: Sono chōsa ni tomonatte, watashi no hō wa waapuro [*word-processor*], sore to pasokon [*personal-computer*] no shijō no ugoki o kenkyū shimashite...

Watanabe: Saisho no miitingu [meeting] desu kara, mina-san ni mo zakkubaran ni hanashite itadakitai to omoimasu.

Chuck: Nihonjin wa enryo-bukai to yoku iwaremasu ga, sore o nori-koete kudasai.

Watanabe: Kaisha ga kakaete iru ookina mondai wa nan deshō ka?

Masuda: **Shain ga nani o kangaete iru ka**, keieisha wa ki ni mo shinai. **Kaisha no taisei wa hijō ni dokusai-teki da to itte ii no de wa nai ka** to kanjimasu.

Itō: **Naze josei ni ochakumi dake de wa naku, motto omoshiroi shigoto o ataenai no ka**, rikai dekimasen. Kurieitibu [creative]-na sainō ga aru no ni...

Tomita: Nani ka mono o tsukuritakereba, kaisha o yamete, **kodomo o tsukureba ii ja nai ka**!

Suzuki: Omae wa damatte ro yo!

Chuck: Shanai-teki-na koto kara maaketingu [market-ing] e wadai o utsushitai to omoimasu kedo....

Masuda: Waapuro [*wodr-processor*] ni taishite **juyō ga aru ka dō ka** o kangaezu ni, sore o tsukuri-tsuzukete iru no wa **hen de wa nai ka** to omoimasu.

Itō: Shōhisha ga **donna mono o motomete iru ka**, sore o kentō shite kara, atarashii shōhin o kaihatsu shinakute wa ikenai.

Suzuki: Mukashi **"Waapuro [*word-processor*] nara, Suzuki no Sumō ja nai to kaitakunai"** to mina ga omotta no ni, ima wareware no burando [brand]-mei wa zenzen wasurarete shimaimashita.

Masuda: **Donna shōhin o kaihatsu suru-beki ka**, soshite sore o **donna fū ni senden suru-beki ka**, kono yō na koto o sekkyokuteki-ni kangaeta ho ga ii no **de wa nai ka** to watashi wa jikkan shite imasu.

Itō: **Watashi wa kaisha ni genki o dō shitara tori-modoseru ka**, to yoku kangaete imasu. Hitsuyō na no wa, chōkikeikaku, sore to **yume de wa nai deshō ka**.

Tomita: Josei nante amachoroi mon' da na. Omae wa Dizuniirando [Disneyland] ni itteereba ii **ja nai ka**?

Itō: Shitsurei shichau! Honne de hanaseba, kaisha ni ichiban songai o ataete iru no wa Tomita-san **de wa nai ka** to mina iimasu yo! **Ano hito ga nokotte te ii no ka** to mina hisoka ni itte imasu yo! Shachō no musume to kekkon shite, zurugashikoi wa!

現場の意見

After concluding their preliminary survey of the company, Chuck and Watanabe are holding a meeting with the staff of Suzuki Denki. They want to hear the opinions of the ordinary employees and use this constructive criticism to redirect the firm. Tomita is sniping away malevolently and destructively in the background.

ワタナベ： まだ早い段階ですが、いろいろな調査をして、社員と話して、なんとか会社の感触を読み取れたといえると思います。

チャック： その調査にともなって、私のほうはワープロ、それとパソコンの市場の動きを研究しまして…

ワタナベ： 最初のミーティングですから、皆さんにもざっくばらんに話していただきたいと思います。

チャック： 日本人は遠慮深いとよく言われますが、それを乗り越えてください。

ワタナベ： 会社が抱えている大きな問題は何でしょうか？

マスダ： 社員が何を考えているか、経営者は気にもしない。会社の体制は非常に独裁的だといっていいのではないかと感じます。

イトウ： なぜ女性にお茶汲みだけではなく、もっと面白い仕事を与えないのか、理解できません。クリエイティブな才能があるのに…

トミタ： 何かものを作りたければ、会社をやめて、子供をつくればいいではないじゃないか！

スズキ： おまえは黙ってろよ！

The Workers Speak Out

チャックさんと渡部さんは、鈴木電気の経営状態及びパソコン市場についての事前調査を終了し、鈴木電気の社員との面接を行っています。会社の独裁的な体制がはっきりしてくると同時に、女性社員に対しての富田副社長の封建的な態度が露出します。

Watanabe: We're still at an early stage of our work, but, after going through a certain amount of data and talking to a number of the employees, I think I've got the general feel of the company.

Chuck: In parallel with Mr. Watanabe's surveys, I've been researching the market trends for word-processors and computers…

Watanabe: Since this is our first meeting, I'd just like everyone to give their opinions in a very free-form, informal way.

Chuck: I know Japanese people are very inhibited, but you've got to overcome that.

Watanabe: So what are the major problems you think this firm has?

Masuda: My feeling is that the managers just don't care **what we think**. I think the way the firm is organized is **a little too autocratic**.

Ms. Ito: What I can't get is **why women can never get to do anything more interesting than making the tea**. I mean, we are creative, but…

Tomita: Hey, if you're so darn creative **why don't you just quit the firm and make some babies!**

Suzuki: Shut up, you!

チャック：	社内的なことからマーケティングへ話題を移したいと思いますけど…
マスダ：	ワープロに対して需要があるかどうかを考えずに、それを造りつづけているのは変ではないかと思います。
イトウ：	消費者がどんなものを求めているか、それを検討してから、新しい商品を開発しなくてはいけない。
スズキ：	昔、「ワープロなら、スズキのスモウじゃないと買いたくない」と皆が思ったのに、今我々のブランド名は全然忘れられてしまいました。
マスダ：	どんな商品を開発するべきか、そしてそれをどんな風に宣伝するべきか、このようなことを積極的に考えたほうが良いのではないかと私は実感しています。
イトウ：	私は会社に元気をどうしたら取り戻せるか、とよく考えています。必要なのは、長期計画、それと夢ではないでしょうか。
トミタ：	女性なんてあまちょろいもんだな。おまえはディズニーランドにいってればいいじゃないか？
イトウ：	失礼しちゃう！本音で話せば、会社に一番損害を与えているのはトミタさんではないかと皆言いますよ！あの人が残ってていいのかと皆ひそかに言っていますよ。社長の娘と結婚して、ずるがしこいわ！

Chuck:	OK, let's switch from the internal side of things to marketing…
Masuda:	I think it's crazy the way that we go on and on making word-processors without ever asking ourselves **if there's demand for them or not.**
Ms. Ito:	I think we've got to first research **what it is that consumers really want**, then develop a new product.
Suzuki:	In the old days people were like "**If I get a word processor, it's got to be a Suzuki Sumo,**" but now our brand name's totally forgotten.
Masuda:	Personally, what I feel is that we ought to think very hard not just about **what products to make**, but then **how we should advertise them**.
Ms. Ito:	I've often thought that **if we want to revive the firm**, what we need is first a long-term plan, then, **surely**, some kind of ideal, or dream.
Tomita:	Women are so sentimental! If you're looking for dreams, **why not go off to Tokyo Disneyland**.
Ms. Ito:	I beg your pardon! Why don't I just say what everybody *really* thinks. It's Tomita, **isn't it**, who's causing the most damage to the firm. You know what everyone says—not openly, of course—that guy shouldn't be allowed to stay in the company. Marrying the boss's daughter. You crafty schemer! Huh!

Know-it-all Notes

• **Nantoka**　なんとか
More or less, in some degree. It is important to scatter such apparently meaningless little expressions throughout your speech in order to sound natural.

• **Kanshoku**　感触
Literally "texture," this word is best rendered *feel* in English. In a country where so little is said directly a sensitivity to "feel" or "atmosphere" is very important.

• **Shimashite**　しまして
This is a slightly more formal form of **shite**.

• **Zakkubaran ni**　ざっくばらんに
This means something like *say what you think when you think without any hesitation.*

• **Enryo-bukai**　遠慮深い
Reserved or *modest.* Chuck, like all Americans familiar with pop-Freudian and pop-Jungian psychology, prefers the more loaded translation *inhibited.*

• **Kakaete iru**　抱えている
This verb almost always goes with **mondai** or something else that is negative, and means something like *to be struggling with, to be burdened with, to be facing.* Learn the phrase **mondai o kakaete iru**.

• **Nan deshō ka**　何でしょうか
Why **deshō**? Because it's oblique, not at all **shitsukoi** (pressing). If one translated the sentiment without regard for the realities of the English language, it would be *If I may ask, what problems might the company have at the moment?*

• Dokusaiteki 独裁的

Dictatorial or *autocratic*. A boss who ultimately decides everything is called a **one-man shachō**.

• Ochakumi お茶汲み

Tea-making. Japanese Office Ladies are nicknamed "**Kaisha no Hana**"—Flowers of the Office: A few years of zero-responsibility jobs then they will be plucked for **shanai-kekkon** (intra-company marriage). In large companies, in addition to providing marriage partners, women also bolster the confidence and self-esteem of the men by being so very manifestly inferior to them. "I may have lost $100 million on that deal in the States, but hey, I do <u>overtime</u>, and I can work a word-processor <u>as well as</u> a kettle and a copy-machine." They are a sort of brain balm, or self-esteem salvage kit, a living-proof to the humiliated and exploited salaryman that he is *not quite* the lowest of the low.

In smaller companies, however, the apparently subordinate women who have less opportunity than the men to waste time in meetings and corrode their brains on drinking sprees are often—like Jeeves the butler—the ones in real control. Recently some companies have started to hire women at the same pay rates to do the same jobs as men. NTT Data, a subsidiary of the telecom giant NTT, now has a policy of recruiting twenty percent women. Ambitious Japanese women tend to be found in foreign companies which are unlikely to be able to recruit suitably-qualified Japanese men and do not discriminate against women.

• Kodomo 子供

Tomita holding the traditional view that women employees should quit by their late twenties to marry and have children, feels that Ito should quit and have a family. If Ito-san stays in the company she runs the risk of being nicknamed an **onibaba** (a devil hag).

• Omae wa damatte ro yo おまえは黙ってろよ！

Shut up you! Being rude in Japanese is not easy, and consists much more in *how* you speak than *what* you say. First, notice that rather than call Tomita by his name, Suzuki calls him **Omae**, a very informal and thus (here) contemptuous form of "you." You must also imagine Suzuki's delivery to be very guttural.

• Hen   変

Translated in the dictionary as *strange*, this adjective has a huge range of meaning from a *teeny-weeny bit odd* to *absolutely insane*. Here, since Masuda is quite rightly criticizing the firm for making things which no one wants anymore, his meaning is probably closer to the latter, strong meaning. This, however, is left to his audience to infer.

• Waapuro nara, Suzuki no Sumō ja nai to kawanai
ワープロなら、スズキのスモウじゃないと買わない

We can see that in the old days Suzuki Denki achieved what Xerox, Hoover, or Jacuzzi did for photocopiers, vacuum cleaners, or whirlpool baths respectively, having their brand name become the generic name for a product.

• Sekkyokutekini   積極的に

Seriously, energetically. He could also have used the adverb shinken ni, which means *earnestly*. For more information on adverbs see Chapter 8.

• Jikkan suru   実感する

Literally, to feel *actually*, perhaps best translated. *I really, strongly feel.* Note also tsūkan suru (lit: feel painfully) *to feel keenly.*

• Genki   元気

In English we can talk of nursing a company back to health, but genki implies more than just the absence of problems, it means *vigorously healthy.*

• Yume   夢

Dream, a more sentimental and humanistic alternative to the slightly megalomaniac "vision," the Japanese *love* this word, which is consequently found littered over advertising campaigns and company slogans. For some examples see the introduction to Chapter 9.

• Zurugashikoi   ずるがしこい

Crafty, cunning, sly. Zurui means *cheat*, and Kashikoi means *clever.*

物知り英語ノート

• **I've got the *feel* of the company**
"会社の雰囲気を読み取れた" 何かを感じる時に使われる **Feel** は、商品の全体的なイメージ、機能を卓越した商品のアピール性を表わす時などに **The *feel* of the product** のようにも使われます。例えば **Coke** は若く、元気でモダンなイメージをアピールしています。

• **In parallel with**
"平行して" **In tandem with／In conjunction with** も同様に使うことができます。

• **A free-form way**
"自由な形に" という意味から "ざっくばらんに" チャックさんと渡部さんは鈴木電気では上下関係が厳しく、自由な発言が許されるような状況でないことに気付いていますが、敢えて **A free-form way** を提案しました。

• **Inhibited**
"遠慮深い" の強い言い方。これより軟らかい言い方をしたければ、**shy, timid**（内気）、**self-effacing**（控えめ）をつかうことができます。反対語は **Uninhibited**。

• **Just don't care**
just はネガティブな気持を強調しています。「ちょっと」という意味だけでなく、ここでは「どうでもいい」を "本当に" と強調するために使われています。

• **Autocratic**
トップダウン組織の "独裁的" 傾向を表わしています。上の者はディスカッションする代わりに命令を下し (**give orders**)、下の者はそれに従う (**obey**) 上下関係が厳しい (**hierarchical**) 軍隊のようなものです。

• Creative
伊藤さんはただのお茶汲みだけでなく、創造的な仕事を求めています。日本に比べてアメリカの男女差別はなくなったといわれますが、**Glass-ceiling**（女性やマイノリティーの人たちはある程度まで出世しても、それ以上は昇進できない）や **Token woman director**（女性差別のない会社の象徴にすぎない女性役員）が残っています。

• Let's switch
話題を変えたい時に使う表現。**Let's turn our attention to ／ Let's move onto** も同じように使うことができます。

• People were like
"皆がそう<u>信じていた</u>、<u>言っていた</u>" という意味で、下線のような動詞の代わりに使われる口語的表現です。

例：**When I saw Ton-chan's eyebrows I was like "are those caterpillars or what?"**
「私はトンちゃんの眉毛を見たとき、毛虫か何かじゃないかと思いました。」
I was like, this is great.
「ぼくはこれは素晴しいと思った。」

• Personally
"個人的には" 自分の個人的な見解を述べる前に使われます。

• I beg your pardon
ここでは "何をいっているんですか" と怒りが込められた言い方です。通常は "失礼ですが" 等丁寧な言い方で使われるのですが、時と場合によって言葉の調子でその意味が変わるという例です。

• What everybody really thinks
日本語の "本音" という単語は、英語では文章で表現するしかありません。

• Schemer
"悪い計画をたてる人" **Scheme** は **Plan** より計略的な意味を含んでいます。

• Crafty
ここで注意したいのは、**Craft** 自体は工芸を意味しますが、**Crafty** は悪賢いを意味する点です。混乱しないようにして下さい。

THREE

●

TOTALLY ARTICULATE THE JOINTS OF LANGUAGE

明確に話すための漠然とした表現

The previous chapter urged you, the reader, to cast off your enslavement to the specious *mot juste* and the static noun, and instead, to switch your allegiance to the simple, but natural and dynamic, verb phrase. Once again, we will encourage you here to resist the temptation to speak wooden, over-formal dictionary Japanese, and learn how effectively a little high-sounding imprecision can lubricate and actually authenticate your language.

Think how often when speaking English we use phrases, such as "*That's the kind of thing we're aiming for*," or "*That's the kind of direction we want to head in*," that if read in cold blood, would seem inexcusably inexact. How many times have you come to the end of a sentence only to find that it lacks the necessary emphasis to officially declare itself as finished? So what do you do? Perhaps, you are forced to conclude with an emphatic commonplace such as "*…and so that's where we stand at the moment*" or "*…basically, that's the state of things now*."

1. THINGS & STUFF
ということ／ところ／もの

● わが社が**目指すところ**は質の高い商品を安く**売ること**です。

Wagasha ga **mezasu tokoro** wa shitsu no takai shōhin o yasuku **uru koto** desu.

What we aim to do is to **sell** quality products at cheap prices.

● 労働費の安さはこの国の唯一いいところだ。

Rōdōhi no yasusa wa kono kuni no yuiitsu **ii tokoro** da.

The only **good thing** about this country is the low labor costs.

● 日本では社員を**解雇すること**はムリです。

Nihon de wa shain o **kaiko suru koto** wa muri desu.

In Japan **firing** people is quite simply not done.

● アメリカで億万長者が多いということは企業家精神に加え市場の大きさというものもあります。

America de **okumanchōja ga ooi to iu koto** wa kigyōkaseishin ni kuwae shijo no ookisa **to iu mono** mo arimasu.

In America **the fact that** there are many super-rich people is definitely related not just to the entrepreneurial spirit, but also to **the factor** of sheer market size.

● 封建的なやり方から脱却して、社員に自由を与えると
　　思いきったものが自然と出てくる。

Hōkenteki-na yarikata kara dakkyaku shite, shain ni
jiyū o ataeru to **omoikitta mono** ga
shizen to dete kuru.

I believe that if you abandon the old-fashioned, feudal way of
doing things and give free rein to your employees,
then that's when **things start to get radical**.

2. CONDITIONS/SITUATIONS/STATES OF AFFAIRS/POINTS/WAYS

具合／状況／現状／点／形／感じ

● 食品メーカーというのは社会の一番重要なところに
　　関わっている。

Shokuhin meekaa [maker] **to iu no wa** shakai no ichiban
jūyō-na tokoro ni kakawatte iru.

A food company , **by definition**, addresses society's most
basic, most fundamental needs.

● 会社は一日で一億円の赤字を出していると
　　いった具合です。

Kaisha wa ichinichi de ichiokuen no akaji o dashite iru
to itta guai desu.

The way things are now we're losing 100 million yen a day!

● 他社と提携するという方向で行こうというのが
　今の状況です。

Tasha to teikei suru **to iu hōkō** de ikō **to iu no ga**
ima no jōkyō desu.

Our present situation is that we're thinking of **developing
along the lines of** making alliances with other firms.

● いくら宣伝しても、いくら値段を下げても、買ってく
　れる人がいないというような状況です。

Ikura senden shite mo, ikura nedan o sagete mo, katte
kureru hito ga inai to iu **yō na jōkyō** desu.

The situation is basically that however much we advertise
and however much we slash prices we still
can't find any buyers.

● なぜ欧米各社の利益率がそんなに高いのか見てみると、
　過剰人員を抱えていない点が重要である。

Naze ōbeikakusha no riekiritsu ga sonna ni takai no ka
mite miru to, kajōjinin o kakaete inai **ten ga jūyō** de aru.

When considering the superior profitability of Western firms,
the fact that they are not burdened with over-manning
is very **significant**.

● 向こうがノーハウを供給し、こっちサイドがハードを
　作るという形で協力していきたい。

Mukō ga nō-hau [know-how] o kyōkyū shi, kocchi saido
[side] ga haado [hard] o tsukuru **to iu katachi** de
kyōryoku shite ikitai.

We want to cooperate **on the basis** that you provide the
know-how, while we make the hardware.

<hr>

3. WAYS/STRUCTURES/OPINIONS/ STAGES/SIDES

方法／構造／味方／考え方／主義／段階／面／の世界

● なるべくたくさんの仕事を下請け会社に回すという
　　　　　　方法しかない。

Narubeku takusan no shigoto o shitauke-gaisha ni
mawasu to iu **hōhō** shika nai.

The only way we can do this is to subcontract out as
much work as possible.

● どうしてもボロ儲けしたい、という欲に基づいた
　　　　構造ができている。

Dōshite mo boromōke shitai to iu yoku ni motozuita
kōzō ga dekite iru.

There's a **whole structure,** mental and social, based upon
the idea of becoming mega-rich.

● リスクを伴うことは、やりたくないという
　見方が普及した。

Risuku [risk] o tomonau koto wa, yaritakunai **to iu mikata** ga fukyū shita.

Not wanting to be involved in anything even remotely risky seems to be the standard **mindset** now.

● サービス中心構造の経済に切り替える時期だという
　考え方は間違っている。

Saabisu [service] chūshin-kōzō no keizai ni kiri-kaeru jiki da **to iu kangaekata** wa machigatte iru.

That whole idea that now is the time to switch to a service based economy is just plain wrong.

● 成長の結果、外国の大手企業に直面する段階になった。

Seichō no kekka, gaikoku no oote-kigyō ni chokumen suru **dankai** ni natta.

In consequence of our growth, we've now reached **the point** where we go head-to-head with the foreign majors.

● 欧米人の私生活重視主義には、生産性と創造性という
　点で、プラス面もある。

Ōbeijin no shiseikatsu-jūshi**shugi** ni wa, seisansei to sōzōsei to iu ten de, **purasu [plus] men** mo aru.

The way Western people put their private life before their work has a **positive impact** on their productivity and creativity.

● 我々は、日本における、マイクロソフト的な
　　存在になりたい。

Wareware wa, Nihon ni okeru, Maikurosofuto [Microsoft]-**teki-na sonzai** ni naritai.

Our aim is to become **a species of** Japanese Microsoft.

● 会議は明日の朝ということで、時間的にはキツイよ。

Kaigi wa ashita no asa to iu koto de, jikan-**teki-ni** wa kitsui yo.

Since the meeting's tomorrow morning, time**wise** things
are pretty tight.

● あの会社のプロジェクトを取れれば、もう数億円の
　　世界ですよ。

Ano kaisha no purojekuto [project] o torereba, mō sūoku-en
no **sekai** desu yo.

If you can pull off a deal with that firm, **you're talking** hun-
dreds of millions of yen.

*in the
neighborhood
of*

AFTERWORD

If you can master the joints of the Japanese language then you
can bend it to say anything you want. The vague little words
introduced in this chapter are therefore one of the most important *things* you'll ever encounter. Remember them and you'll
be able to say lots of *stuff*. **That's the point I want to emphasize!**

Schedule no setsumei

Chuck: Ima made, shain to mensetsu shitari, kaisha no shiryō ya kaikei nado o mitari, iroiro-na kakudo kara onsha ga kakaete iru mondai o chōsa shite kimashita. **Deeta [data] o atsumeru koto** ga owatte, watashi-tachi no konsarutingu-saabisu [consultant service] wa ima kara **bunseki no dankai** ni hairimasu.

Watanabe: Raishū no nakaba gurai ni, korekara kaisha o dō iu hōkō ni tenkai suru-beki ka, futari de purezen [*presen*tation] o okonaimasu. **Purezen [*presen*tation] to iu no wa, kōgi mitai-na mono** de wa naku, watashi-tachi ga iroiro iken o nobetari, adobaisu [advice] o shitari, onsha no shain mo sore ni taishite jibun no iken o ieru, to iu jiyū-na katachi no miitingu [meeting] ni shitai. Tsumari kōgi to iu yori, **iken-kōkan ni chikai mono** ni narimasu.

Tomita: Mina de **kaisha no mondai to sono kaiketsu-hōhō o hanashi-au to iu wake** desu ka?

Chuck: Ee, **sō iu kanji** desu.

Tomita: **Chuck-san to Watanabe-san ga mezasu toko-ro** ga nan na no ka, chotto rikai shigatai desu ne. Wareware wa, Nihon ni irun' desu yo! Wareware wa Nihonjin desu yo! Ganbatte, harikitte mondai o nori-koerun' desu yo!

Sō iu "jiyū-na katachi no miitingu [meeting],"
Sonna **Beverly Hills-teki-na** seishin-chiryō nan
te irimasen. Maru de **Woody Allen no sekai** ja
nai no?

Chuck: **Enryo naku hanashi-au koto** ni, **mainasu
[minus]-men** ga aru to omoenai. **Kokoro o
mina ni uchi-akeru koto** wa **Amerika-teki** to iu
yori ningen-teki de wa nai desu ka? Kyōryoku,
shin'yō, **sonkei o shiau koto**, **konna koto** ga
kaisha no kaifuku no kagi o nigitte irun' desu.

スケジュールの説明

Having now, in addition to document-based research, spoken to both management and the ordinary employees, the consultants of McVitie finally feel ready to start developing their strategy for the revitalization of Suzuki Denki. They announce when they will hold their first presentation-cum-discussion, but the ever uncooperative Tomita appears to object to their methods as "un-Japanese."

チャック： 今まで、社員と面接したり、会社の資料や会計などを見たり、いろいろな角度から御社が抱えている問題を調査してきました。データを集めることが終わって、私たちのコンサルティングサービスはいまから分析の段階に入ります。

ワタナベ： 来週の半ばぐらいに、これから会社をどういう方向に展開するべきか、二人でプレゼンを行います。プレゼンというのは、講義みたいなものではなく、私たちがいろいろ意見を述べたり、アドバイスをしたり、御社の社員もそれに対して自分の意見を言える、という自由な形のミーティングにしたい。つまり講義というより、意見交換に近いものになります。

トミタ： 皆で会社の問題とその解決方法を話し合うというわけですか。

チャック： ええ、そういう感じです。

トミタ： チャックさんと渡部さんが目指すところが何なのか、ちょっと理解し難いですね。我々は、日本にいるんですよ。我々は日本人ですよ。頑張って、張り切って問題を乗り越えるんですよ。そういう「自由な形のミーティング」、そんなビバーリーヒルズ的な精神治療なんていらない。まるでウッディー・アレンの世界じゃないの？

Explaining the Project Schedule

鈴木電気の抱える問題点を調査した結果、今後どのような方向を目指すべきかをプレゼンテーションし、社員全員で問題点の解決方法を検討したいと提案するチャックさんと渡部さんに、封建社会で生まれ育ったような富田副社長はアメリカ的な方法に難色を示します。

Chuck: Up till now we've been investigating the problems that your company is grappling with from a number of different angles, by interviewing employees, examining documentation, accounts and so forth. Now that **the data-gathering part of things** is complete, our consulting will move on **to the analytical level**.

Watanabe: About the middle of next week we intend to make a joint-presentation on **what direction** the company should develop in. **When we say presentation** we don't mean **a kind of lecture**, we mean a freeform meeting in which we will put forward our opinions and give advice, after which you can express your opinions too. In short, rather than a lecture it will be **a sort of exchange of ideas**.

Tomita: **You mean** we're all going to talk about the company's problems and how to solve them?

Chuck: **That's the idea**, yes.

Tomita: I find it a little hard to understand exactly **what it is** you gentlemen are aiming for. We are in Japan! We are Japanese! We overcome problems by persevering, by never giving up! We don't need this kind of "freeform meeting," this **Beverly Hills-style** psychotherapy. **It's like a Woody Allen movie!**

チャック： 遠慮なく話し合うことにマイナス面があるとは思えない。心を皆に打ち明けることはアメリカ的というより人間的ではないですか？協力、信用、尊敬しあうこと、こんなことが会社の回復の鍵を握っているんです。

Chuck: I don't see **anything bad** about **opening up to one another**. Surely **telling people what you really think** is not so much American as just plain human. **To** cooperate with one another, **to** trust one another, **to** respect one another, **these are the kind of things** that hold the key to this company's recovery!

Know-it-all Notes

• Mensetsu   面接

Literally *"face contact,"* mensetsu is now used almost exclusively for job interviews and as part of the admission procedure for schools and colleges. It carries the implication that both parties are meeting *face-to-face* for the first time. For interviews appearing in magazines, newspapers, and TV programs, remember the following rule: **journalist + non-famous person = shuzai, journalist + celebrity = interview,** and **celebrity (or well-known journalist) + celebrity = taidan.**

• Nakabagurai   半ばぐらい

About the middle of next week. Note also raishū no atamagurai (about the beginning of next week) and raishū no owarigurai (about the end of next week). Other expressions of approximate time which it may be as well to know would be chōjun, chūjun, gejun referring to the beginning, middle, and end of a month respectively.

• Okonaimasu   行います

An all purpose word meaning basically "to do" but with the magisterial air of *to carry out* or *to conduct.* Use it.

• Purezen   プレゼン

Here, the English word *presentation* has been reduced to a mere three syllables in Japanese. We have also seen *restructure* become risutora, and a more comic example is provided by the misleading buresto, the Japanese word for *brainstorming.* In fact, this is a common way to abbreviate both borrowed and native words in the Japanese language. Whereas English speakers seem happy to make acronyms—UN, RADAR, etc, Japanese prefer to omit unnecessary phonetic units from polysyllabic words. The eight-syllable jidōhanbaiki (vending machine), for example, is often halved to the more dynamic jihanki. No word or expression, it seems, is too great to escape extensive cutting, even

*Hashi*moto *Ryu*taro, the present prime minister, has been nicknamed "Hashi Ryu" by the popular press.

• Tsumari つまり

Basically, in short. Use this to sum up what you've been saying, or to cut your losses when you've lost the thread of what you've said and want to escape with dignity.

• Hanashi-au 話し合う

Talk through, thrash out. The ending -au indicates reciprocity. In Ginza neon signs of FujiFilm and Kodak stand opposite one another. We could say Ginza de Fuji to Kodak no neon wa niramiatte iru. *The neon signs of Kodak and Fuji are giving one another the eye in Ginza.*

• Chotto rikai shigatai ちょっと理解し難い

A little hard to understand. By being excessively polite Tomita is making clear his contempt for Chuck and Watanabe's proposal. This kind of insulting phoney politeness is called inginburei.

• Ganbatte 頑張って

From here Tomita gives the classic view of the Japanese on the Japanese. No shortcuts, no tricks, if you work hard, if you put in the hours, if you slave all the way to the knacker's yard (like Boxer the horse in *Animal Farm* with his motto "I will work harder"), ultimately you will triumph. Discussion or re-thinking are namby-pamby, a symptom of the kibenshakai (society of sophistry) that some henkutsu oyaji (grumpy old geezers) chose to regard the United States as having become. The way the Japanese regard themselves and the Americans is similar to the way in which the Romans regarded the Greeks. *They talk, we do. They are all words, we are all action.* See Virgil, *Aeneid* VI, 847-853.

Time magazine had a cover depicting the United States as a baby in stars and stripes diapers to illustrate that the Japanese just regard the Americans with their complaints about closed markets and dumping as so many cry-babies!

• **Woody Allen**　ウッディー・アレン

No doubt archetype New Yorker and movie director, Woody Allen will take offense to his name being mentioned in the same breath as Beverly Hills, a locale satirized in his 1974 Oscar-winning classic *Annie Hall*. How does Tomita know about Woody Allen? Perhaps he has read the gossip in the tabloid press—*Nikan Gendai* and *Yukan Fuji*—that he buys at the station kiosk each evening to check the racing results, read the porno pages, and reinforce his *hoshu-teki* (conservative) ways.

• **Kagi o nigitte iru**　鍵を握っている

Holds the key to. An idiomatic expression that is identical in Japanese and English.

物知り英語ノート

- **Grappling with**

"取り組む"。代わりに **Struggling with／faced with** を使用することもできます。

- **Documentation**

"様々な資料、文章" という意味で使われる集合名詞です。

- **And so forth**

意味は **Etcetera** と同じですが、言葉の響きがよく感じられます。

- **When we say presentation, we (don't) mean…**

プレゼンテーション<u>というのは</u>、という日本語を英訳するときには日本語よりも説明的な文章となります。

- **In short**

"つまり、ひとことでいえば" 要約して物事を話す時につかわれます。

- **That's the idea**

yes に頼りすぎず、潤いのある表現で **agreement** （同意）を表わしています。

- **I find it _a little_ hard to understand _exactly_ what it is you _gentlemen_ are aiming for**

下線のように丁寧すぎる言葉を使いながら、実際には富田さんはマクビティー社の社員を馬鹿にしています。

- **We are in Japan!**

レトリック上のトリックです。富田さんは、前の文章では非常に丁寧な回りくどい言い方をしておきながら、突然、その言い回しを変えダイレクトな話し方をしています。

- **Beverly Hills**

精神科医に通うことが日常生活の一部となっている、クリエイティブな仕事をしている大金持ちが、大勢住んでいる街といえるでしょう。

• Woody Allen movie

結婚問題や男女間の問題に直面しているカップルに焦点をあて、彼等がとことん話し合う場面が多い、聞きがいのある作品を作り出す監督です。昔気質の富田さんにとっては、男は黙ってじっと我慢という生き方が普通であり、思っていることを自由に話し合うという行為が卑しく見えるようです。

• Just plain human

<u>ただの、たんなる</u>という **just** を用いて、"人間そのものだ、人間の本質だ" という意味を強調しています。

例：**He's not a clever businessman, he's just a plain crook**
「彼は優秀なビジネスマンではなく、ただの詐欺師だ」

FOUR

●

KATAKANA KATAPULT
BINGE ON BUZZWORDS

ボーダレスワード：外来語パワー

There may not be an *Academie Nipponaise* to guard the purity of the Japanese language, but it is a fact that the everyday use of katakana loan words in the business world is very successfully concealed from the average foreign student. While many textbooks for beginners aim to encourage by disingenuously pretending that students can perfect their Japanese simply by stringing together words such as **beer**, **tabaco**, **snack** and **table**, no one has pointed out that learning a few katakana loan words of a more abstract and flexible kind can miraculously propel students from halting, limping speech to highly idiomatic vernacular Japanese.

OVERCOME YOUR INHIBITIONS

The most important thing to do before strapping yourself into the katakana katapult is to overcome any hang-ups about using "English" words in Japanese. You must not imagine that every time you use a katakana loan word your audience is sniggering at your ignorance of the *pure* Japanese alternative. (*Pure*

Japanese kanji, after all, were imported wholesale from China!) Katakana loan words are not a dishonorable and cowardly escape-hatch from *real* Japanese. They are a significant and valid part of the evolving language, often with shades of meaning quite distinct from their *apparently* interchangeable kanji synonym.

One crucial tip to get optimum performance and maximum enjoyment from the katakana katapult. If embarrassment forces you to retain native pronounciation when using loan words in Japanese you'll mess up your speech-rhythms and most likely be unintelligible to the Japanese listener: mis-pronounce them with uninhibited enthusiasm and they'll turn into real Japanese, and you into a real Japanese businessman!

1. APPEAR DYNAMIC & DECISIVE

Katakana *is* dynamic: More *things* can be expressed in *fewer words*. Indeed it could be regarded as the verbal equivalent of miniaturization, a species of micro-language! Imeeji up suru (*to improve one's image, experience a dramatic rise in status*), for example, would require many more words to be rendered in either *proper* Japanese or English. Judicious use of katakana, however, can make the speaker seem brisk, decisive, and vigorous. Bosses of electronics, computer, retail, and advertising companies may speak up to thirty percent katakana! Up to seventy percent of their "big ideas" may be expressed in katakana! Note that the most conservative (and least honest?) sections of the Japanese establishment use very little katakana, preferring to conceal sins ranging from fear of foreign competition to bribery and corruption behind a heavy and multilayered curtain of circumlocutory super-polite language. Katakana is for those who wish to cut the Gordian knot.

2. INSTANT TOM PETERS-SAN

Katakana, far from implying that a speaker is incapable of speaking Japanese, suggests that he has learned everything there is to learn in Japan and, mentally at least, has ranged abroad, picked up the latest trends from American business schools, and then (rather as the Health Ministry does with imported perfume) slightly modified the contents to suit local consumer tastes. Katakana English business terminology is non-threatening, *domesticated* American business philosophy, aggressive management science with its claws pulled.

Katakana can thus confer instant *cosmopolitan business guru status*, without making the speaker appear threateningly foreign and different. The more katakana you know, the wiser you are, and, on occasion, the more your audience are forced to rely on you to explain it for them. Skilful use of katakana can help establish a power-relationship with you in the driving seat. If someone tries to browbeat you with a word like リスト ラ **ristra** (*restructuring*), why don't you pull out your パラダイム シフト (*paradigm shift*) and show him who's boss!

3. HOW TO MAKE JOKES, MAKE FRIENDS, AND INFLUENCE PEOPLE

Katakana can be purely humorous. Perhaps based on the preconception that all foreigners are very large and very loud and very indiscreet, katakana has a kind of implicit ham-actor facetious quality, a built-in wink and nudge. Thus if you were to say to a beautiful office lady **"Totemo utsukushii nikutai desu ne"** (*What a beautiful meat-body you have*) the threatening implication would be something smutty like "I want to jump your bones." If, however, you substituted the katakana expression ダイナマイトバディ (dynamite body), something perilously close to sexual harassment would metamorphose into an outdated, overblown and humorous remark.

The example sentences are divided into three groups, **1.** sentences based on katakana verb phrases with **suru**, **2.** sentences based on katakana verb phrases with verbs other than **suru** (e.g: **okonau, naru, ukeru** etc.), and **3.** sentences based on katakana abstract terms (such as *balance, mechanism, trend* etc.)

1. VERB PHRASES WITH SURU
動詞 1

● キーボードアレルギーを抱えているあのオヤジは、まだパソコンをマスターしていない。

Kiibōdo-arerugii [keyboard allergy] o kakaete iru ano oyaji wa, mada **pasokon [*pers*onal *com*puter]** o **masutaa [master]** shite inai.

That old guy who suffers from "**computer-phobia**" still hasn't mastered his PC.

● 中国がいつ経済的にアメリカにキャッチアップするのか、それは21世紀のキーポイントだよ。

Chūgoku ga itsu keizaiteki-ni **Amerika** ni **kyacchi-appu [catch up]** suru no ka, sore wa nijūsseiki no **kiipointo [keypoint]** dayo.

When is China going to catch up with America economically, that is the big question to be answered in the twenty-first century.

- もうちょっとプッシュしたら、契約をとれる
  という印象を受けた。

Mō chotto **pusshu** [push] shitara, keiyaku o toreru
to iu inshō o uketa.

My impression was that if you just **persevered**
a little more, you could get the contract.

- 営業戦士のガンバリズムというのは、ギブアップ
  しないということですよ。

Eigyō-senshi no ganbarizumu to iu no wa, **gibu-appu**
[give up] shinai to iu koto desu yo.

What is the nature of the company-footsoldier's
courage? Never to **give up**!

- 社内情報システムをグレードアップしないかぎり、
  ホワイトカラーの生産性を向上できない。

Shanai-jōhō **shisutemu** [system] o **gureedo-appu**
[grade up] shinai kagiri, **howaito-karaa** [white
collar] no seisansei o kōjō dekinai.

If you don't **improve** the internal information **systems**,
there's no way you can increase **white-collar** productivity.

- 半導体業界をリードしているのはインテルだ。

Handōtai-gyōkai o **riido** [lead] shite iru no wa
Interu [Intel] da.

It's Intel who **lead** the field in semiconductors.

● コストダウンを狙うとき、クローズアップされるのは
中間管理職です。

Kosuto-daun [costdown] o nerau toki, **kurōzu-appu
[close up]** sareru no wa chūkankanrishoku desu.

When looking to **cut costs**, it's middle-managers whose
role **really gets scrutinized**.

● DM、それと飛び込み電話をフォローしないと、
セールスは出来ない。

DM, sore to tobi-komi denwa o **forō [follow]** shinai to,
seerusu [sales] wa dekinai.

If you don't **follow** through on your **direct mail shots** and
cold calls, you'll never **sell** anything.

● ロゴを変えて、オリンピックのスポンサーになって、
会社全体がイメージアップした。

Rogo [logo] o kaete, Orinpikku [Olympic] no **suponsaa
[sponsor]** ni natte, kaishazentai ga **imeeji-appu
[image up]** shita.

In consequence of changing our **logo** and becoming one of the
sponsors of the Olympics, our corporate **image
improved** dramatically.

2. VERB PHRASES WITH VERBS OTHER THAN **SURU**

動詞 2

● 「大企業病にかかった会社に、チャレンジしよう！」と
いうシリコンバレー的マインドを持つべきです。

"Daikigyō-byō ni kakatta ano kaisha ni, **charenji [challenge]**
shiyō!" to iu **shirikon-baree [silicon valley]**-teki
maindo [mind] o motsu-beki desu.

From now on we've got to **think** like those **Silicon Valley**
guys—"let's take on those lethargic, monster firms."

● コンサルタントのギャラに関して、なにか
トラブルがあって、そのプロジェクトは
ペンディングになった。

Konsarutanto [consultant] no **gyara [_guara_ntee]** ni
kanshite, nani ka **toraburu [trouble]** ga atte,
sono **purojekuto [project]** wa **pendingu
[pending]** ni natta.

There was some **problem** about the **consultant's fee**.
As a result the **project's** been **put on hold**.

● やっとマーケティング部とアポイントをとれた。
これからサクセスストーリーが始まるぞ。

Yatto **maaketingu [marketing]**-bu to **apointo [appoint]**
o toreta. Korekara **sakusesu-sutōrii [success
story]** ga hajimaru zo.

At last I managed to get an **appointment** with their **marketing**
division. This is where we **really take off**!

- 社長は全社員にインスピレーションを与える
  ビジョンを持つべきだ。

**Shachō wa zenshain ni insupireeshon [inspiration] o
ataeru bijon [vision] o motsu-beki da.**

It's the duty of the boss to have a **vision** that can
inspire all the staff.

- 世界経済のグローバル化に伴って、我々も
  アジアシフトを進めています。

**Sekai-keizai no gurōbaru [global]-ka ni tomonatte, ware-
ware mo Ajia-shifuto [Asia shift] o susumete imasu.**

In step with the **globalization** of the world economy, we are
shifting our focus to **Asia**.

to advance
put forward

- インターネット時代において英語力はメジャーな
  プラスになる。

**Intaanetto [internet]-jidai ni oite eigoryoku wa mejaa
[major]-na purasu [plus] ni naru.**

In the era of the **Internet**, English ability is a **major plus**.

- マツダのボンゴフレンディーという車名には、ある
  意味でインパクトがあることは否定できない。

**Matsuda no Bongo Furendii to iu shamei ni wa, aru imi de
inpakuto [impact] ga aru koto wa hitei dekinai.**

It can't be denied that Mazda's car name "Bongo Friendee"
has a certain **striking quality**.

3. ABSTRACT "CONCEPT" TERMS
用途の広い抽象名詞

● 調和のとれた、つまりバランスのいい会社を目指したい。

Chōwa no toreta, tsumari **baransu [balance]**
no ii kaisha o mezashitai.

We want to become a harmonious, by that I mean,
a **well-balanced** company.

● 若者の中で、会社人間になりたくなくてフリーター
ライフをチョイスするトレンドが目立つ。

Wakamono no naka de, kaisha-ningen ni naritakunakute
furiitaa-raifu [free*ter*-life] o **choisu [choice]** suru
torendo [trend] ga medatsu.

Among young people one striking **trend** is to reject the
corporate straitjacket and **choose** a **life of
short-term, temporary jobs**.

● ビジネスをスムーズに進めるためには、政治家に
ワイロを払うしかない時もある。

Bijinesu [business] o **sumūzu [smooth]** ni susumeru tame
ni wa, seijika ni wairo o harau shika nai toki mo aru.

Sometimes to make your **business** run **smoothly** you have no
choice but to bribe a politician.

● 意思決定の過程をスピード化すること、それが再生の
　キーポイント。

Ishi-kettei no katei o **supiido [speed]**-ka suru koto, sore ga
saisei no **kiipointo [keypoint]**.

Speeding up the decision-making process is the **key** to
reviving the firm.

● アメリカで日本車を作ろうというコンセプトをベース
　に、GMはサターンを開発した。

Amerika de Nihonsha o tsukurō to iu **konseputo [concept]**
o **beesu [base]** ni, GM wa Saturn o kaihatsu shita.

Based on the **concept** of producing a Japanese car in the **US**,
GM developed the Saturn.

● 一日で4万人が解雇されたあの会社で、モラルが
　低下するのは当然のことだ。

Ichinichi de yon-man-nin ga kaiko sareta ano kaisha de
moraru [morale] ga teika suru no wa tōzen no koto da.

At that firm where they just fired 40,000 people in a single day,
the fact that **morale** is at rock-bottom is hardly a surprise.

naturally

● このシステムには使いやすさというメリットがあります。

Kono **shisutemu [system]** ni wa tsukai yasusa to iu
meritto [merit] ga arimasu.

This system has the great **merit** of being easy to use.

● インターネットをどのように宣伝のツールに利用できる
　のかを、研究しています。

Intaanetto [internet] o dono yō ni senden no **tsūru [tool]**
ni riyō dekiru no ka o, kenkyū shite imasu.

> We're investigating how we can exploit the
> **Internet** as a PR **tool**.

● 奇蹟なんてなかった。自己主義よりチームワークを
　大事にしながら、頑張っただけだ。

Kiseki nante nakatta. Jikoshugi yori **chiimuwaaku [team-
work]** o daiji ni shinagara, ganbatta dake da.

> Miracle? There was no miracle. Everyone just worked hard,
> like **teamplayers**, not just obsessing about themselves.

● 使い捨てカメラはいま日本でブームになっています。

Tsukaisute kamera wa ima Nihon de **būmu [boom]**
ni natte imasu.

> Film-with-lens cameras are **booming** in Japan.

● 最初売れなくても、私たちはこの技術に100%コミット
　しています。

Saisho urenakutemo, watashitachi wa kono gijutsu ni
100% **komitto [commit]** shite imasu.

> Even if it doesn't take off immediately, we are one-hundred
> percent **committed** to this technology.

Business yōgo taikai

Chuck: Suzuki Denki wa korekara chōyūryō-kigyō o mezashite hoshii!

Watanabe: Chuck-san ga iitai no wa, Suzuki Denki wa **ekuserento-kanpanii [excellent company]** ni naru koto o **gōru [goal]** ni shinakereba naranai to iu koto?

Chuck: Ee. Tomita to Suzuki-shachō ga kenka bakari shite iru no de, shain no yaruki ga nakunatta...

Watanabe: Chuck-san ga iitai no wa, **vaitaritii [vitality] no aru** kaisha ja nai to dame to iu koto?

Chuck: Ee, Sō iu kanji. Yappari, kaisha ni genki no nai koto ga **shōhin-sekkei**, sore to **shōhin-mei**, **utai-monku**, tsumari **senden-hōhō zentai** o **tsumaranai mono** ni shite iru.

Watanabe: Moshikashite, Chuck-san ga iitai no wa, kaisha no **moraru [morale]** ga **daun [down]** shite iru koto de shōhin no **dezain [design]**, **neemingu [naming]**, **surōgan [slogan]**, subete no **PR**-teki-na mono ga **apiiru [appeal]**-sei no nai mono ni natte iru?

Chuck: Monojitai ga ii kedo, **kōkoku** ga yori **inshō-teki de nai** to urenai ne.

Watanabe: Yō suru ni, **inpakuto [impact]** no aru **maaketingu [marketing]** ga atta hō ga **betaa [better]** to iu koto?

Chuck: Ee, **sekai-senjutsu** o kangaeru to IBM ya Gillette mitai ni, **ittaika shita seisaku** ga hitsuyō da.

Watanabe: **Gurōbaru-burando-sutoratejii [global brand strategy]** no koto desu ka?

Chuck: Tomita-san wa **ookina yume** o motenai yatsu da. Zettai ni sore ni hantai suru deshō ne?

Watanabe: Tashika-ni, aitsu ni **bijon [vision]** wa nai. Ano hito ga inakereba, **risutora [restructure]** ga **smūzu [smooth]** ni ugoku no ni... zannen nagara Nihon de wa kare mitai-na **eriito-kōsu [elite course]** o susunda hito o kubi ni suru koto wa ichiō **tabū [taboo]** dakara naa...

Chuck: **Baburu [bubble]** keizai, jūsen-mondai, subete ano **eriito [elite]** renchū no sei da!

Watanabe: Kimari da! Ano hito o **danpingu [dumping]** shiyō!

ビジネス用語大会

Chuck is giving his views on the main problems besetting Suzuki Denki. He is proudly parading his pure and polysyllabic Japanese, but is forever being corrected by Watanabe who prefers a simpler and more practical, if somewhat mongrelized, katakana-rich mode of speech. As ever, the sinister specter of Tomita floats poisonously over the dialogue which concludes with a curse upon him and all the university elite.

チャック：　鈴木電気はこれから超優良企業を目指してほしい！

ワタナベ：　チャックさんが言いたいのは、鈴木電気はエクセレントカンパニーになることをゴールにしなければならないということ？

チャック：　ええ。富田と鈴木社長がけんかばかりしているので、社員のやる気がなくなった…

ワタナベ：　チャックさんが言いたいのは、ヴァイタリティーのある会社じゃないとダメということ？

チャック：　ええ、そういう感じ。やっぱり、会社に元気のないことが商品設計、それと商品名、歌い文句、つまり宣伝方法全体をつまらないものにしている。

ワタナベ：　もしかして、チャックさんが言いたいのは、会社のモラルがダウンしていることで商品のデザイン、ネーミング、スローガン、すべてのPR的なものがアピール性のないものになっている？

チャック：　もの自体が良いけど、広告がより印象的でないと売れないね。

ワタナベ：　要するに、インパクトのあるマーケティングがあったほうがベターということ？

Consultants' Jargon-fest

チャックさんが鈴木電気の問題点に対する個人的意見を述べていますが、クールなビジネス英語を使いこなす渡部さんには、チャックさんの英語が古く色あせたものに感じるようです。（日本語の商品名称を最近ではブランドネーミングという方が一般的ですが、このようなイメージの違いがふたりの言葉の間にあります。）

Chuck: I want Suzuki Denki to aim to be a *truly outstanding business.*

Watanabe: Do you mean, you want Suzuki Denki to set itself **the goal** of becoming an "**excellent company**?"

Chuck: Yes. With Tomita and Suzuki, the CEO, just fighting all the time the employees have lost *their enthusiasm for work.*

Watanabe: You mean that if the firm doesn't have **spark and vitality**, then it's as good as finished?

Chuck: Yeah, that's right. The company's *overall lack of energy* results in *unexciting product specifications, unexciting product names, unexciting catchphrases.* Basically their *whole communications platform* is *uninspiring.*

Watanabe: Are you trying to say that since the employees' **morale** is **low**, **product design**, **naming**, **advertising slogans**—I mean all the **PR**—is totally **unsexy**, completely without **appeal**?

Chuck: The products themselves are good, but if the *advertisements* aren't more *impressive*, their stuff just won't sell.

Watanabe: In short, it would be better if they had more **striking marketing**.

チャック：　　　ええ。世界戦術を考えると、IBMやGilletteみたいに、一体化した政策が必要だ。

ワタナベ：　　　グローバル・ブランド・ストラテジーのことですか？

チャック：　　　富田さんは大きな夢を持てない奴だ。絶対それに反対するでしょうね？

ワタナベ：　　　確かに、あいつにビジョンはない。あの人がいなければ、リストラがスムーズにいくのに…残念ながら日本では彼みたいなエリートコースを進んだ人を首にすることは一応タブーだからなあ…

チャック：　　　バブル経済、住専問題、すべてあのエリート連中のせいだ。

ワタナベ：　　　きまりだ！あの人をダンピングしよう！

Chuck: Yes, when thinking of a *worldwide business plan*, like IBM or Gillette *a consistent policy* is essential.

Watanabe: Are you referring to a **unified global brand strategy**?

Chuck: But the problem is Mr. Tomita is the kind of person unable to *dream great dreams*. He's bound to oppose us, don't you think?

Watanabe: Sure, that guy's got no **vision** whatsoever. If he weren't there, the whole **restructuring** would run real **smoothly**... But, unfortunately in Japan it's **taboo** to fire **graduates from elite universities** like him.

Chuck: But it's guys exactly like him who caused the bubble economy and the housing loan problem.

Watanabe: OK. That's decided then. Let's **dump** him!

Know-it-all Notes

• Excellent Company   エクセレントカンパニー

This phrase was popularized by Tom Peters and Robert Waterman Jr.'s classics *In Search of Excellence* and *A Passion for Excellence*, both of which were written in response to a crisis of confidence in American management techniques provoked by the unstoppable success of the Japanese in the 1970s.

Peters and Waterman castigated scientific and rational managers who did everything by the book while lacking any feel for the product. They found that the "excellent" American companies had certain common features: To encourage lots of communication, to place irrational emphasis on customer service and quality, to treat all the staff as valuable individuals who worked better the more responsibility they were given, and to aim for a general "looseness" in the organization to maximize the occurrence of creative accidents.

• Shōhin-sekkei/shōhinmei/utai-monku/senden-hōhō
商品設計／商品名／歌い文句／宣伝方法

Like many over-eager foreigners, Chuck is trying desperately to speak "Japanese" Japanese. Of these four words shōhinmei and senden-hōhō are fine as they are, but shōhin-sekkei instead of dezain [design], and utai-monku for surogan [slogan] are very awkward, anachronistic, smelling-of-the-dictionary words. Have the courage to ignore foreigners or Japanese not connected with business who correct your katakana-Japanese to apparently *pure* Japanese.

• No hō ga Better   のほうがベター

You've heard of a double negative, but probably not of a "double comparative." Here the -er is provided once in Japanese (no hō ga) and once in English too. Katakana usually has no respect for the language from which it borrows. Consider the expression mai-peesu [my pace] of which the pronoun never changes regardless of the subject, or the movie title *Last of the Mohicans*, modified to *Last of Mohican* (losing an article and a plural) in Japanese.

• Sekai-senjutsu   世界戦術

Here Chuck in his enthusiasm for pure Japanese has made a gaff. The word **sekai-senjutsu** (1) predates consumer society and (2) has overtones of 1930s militarism which make it unpopular in contemporary Japan. Watanabe's **Global (brand) Strategy** is therefore more idiomatic Japanese.

• Elite course o susunda hito   エリートコースを進んだ人

This expression refers to those who have graduated from the most distinguished universities like Keio and Tokyo into government ministries, the great trading companies, or top-level manufacturers.

• Jūsen-mondai   住専問題

The Housing Loan Problem. The Housing Loan Corporations managed largely by former Ministry of Finance officials lent colossal sums of money to shady property developers in the early 1990s. By 1995, they were left with $695 billion of non-performing loans that the taxpayer was called upon to cover.

An MOF official appeared on TV explaining that since this sum would require a tax hike, everyone would have to work harder to pay more tax, thus the whole thing was not a problem but (by a roundabout route) a stimulus to the economy!

• Renchū   連中

A word meaning **nakama** or *group*, this here suggests an "old-boy network" for their mutual benefit while completely ignoring their appointed responsibilities.

• Dumping   ダンピング

Originally meaning "to sell below cost price in foreign markets," Watanabe is here using it to mean *to dump* or *to get rid of*, something he can do thanks to having been educated in the US. The Japanese love puns and wordplay and we urge our readers to approach katakana with a *Wayne's World* attitude: Play with Japanese in the same way that Wayne played with the word "babe" to make *Babarama, Babraham Lincoln*, etc.

物知り英語ノート

• Excellent company

1982年トム・ピーターズとロバート・ウォーターマン・JRによる著書で有名になった "超優良企業" の意味です。両著者は過去20年間の環境の変化に高い適応力を持つ企業と革新的なアメリカの優良企業を分析し、その優秀さを紹介すると共に、どのように日本企業と戦うかを記しています。

• Overall lack of energy

"全体的なエネルギーの欠乏"。上層部がうまく働いていない鈴木電気のような会社では、社員にもその影響が及んでしまいます。これは次の例文のように使われます。

Considered as individuals they are all well-qualified and experienced, but overall there's something missing.

「個人的には素晴しい資格や経歴を持っているのですが、全体的に何か欠けています」

• Unexciting

"面白くない"。チャックさんは鈴木電気の上層部がうまく機能していないことが unexciting product specifications（商品設計）、unexciting product names（商品名）、unexciting catchphrases（キャッチフレーズ）を作り出していると考えています。

• Unexciting product names

全世界のPC市場を目指す鈴木電気においては、日本国内でしか通じない「相撲」のようなブランド名は、世界に通じるものに変更したほうがよいでしょう。グローバルブランドを確立することは、経済的にも大きな効果をもたらします。

• Dump

"投棄する，降ろす"。ここではダンプカーが車を傾けて荷物を投げ下ろすように、富田さんを会社から追い出すという意味で使われています。日本語のダイアログで渡部さんが本来、海外市場への商品の投げ売りを意味するダンピングという外来語を使っている点に注目して下さい。

FIVE

•

PERSUASIVE PRESENTATIONS
&
COMPELLING CHARTS

プレゼンをパワー・アップ！

According to one of the commonplaces of Nihonjinron (the study of Japanese*ness*) the Japanese are so homogenous that they do not even require to speak in order to transmit their thoughts to one another. The head tilted to a certain, significant angle, a distinct pattern of furrows on the brow, the sudden intake of breath at a specific velocity, the explosive coughing fit—these are the means, apparently, by which communication is achieved.

Whether or not one regards such pseudo-anthropological mumbo-jumbo as no more than the whitewashing of inarticulacy, it is important (for the preservation of one's sanity) to recognize that, while the guileless reader may associate the word "meeting" with such actions as *the clear statement of a point of view, the balanced discussion of pros and cons*, all culminating in *the reaching of a decision,* the prefixing of the adjective "Japanese" makes such preconceptions quite invalid.

That the only thing more impressive than the high productivity of the Japanese factory is the prodigiously low productivity of the Japanese office is now a trite observation. It can, however, be helpful to regard the Japanese meeting as the most exquisite expression of the (otherwise repressed) natural urge to be unproductive: An opportunity joyfully seized by an excessively virtuous and diligent nation to waste time, and go round in circles, rather than quality circles. With Japanese business the gestation period for any decision is elephantine, and the meeting is no more than a prenatal breathing exercise for a birth that will take place years hence!

An examination of some expressions related to meetings, shows us that reaching a swift decision is not the end in mind. **Kao o awaseru**, (to put one's faces together) is no more than a sniffing at the spoor. **Hara no saguriai**, (the mutual feeling-out of the stomachs) could perhaps be likened to the salt-flinging, thigh-slapping, and glaring of Sumo wrestlers prior to the bout.

In Japan one finds some curiously paradoxical concepts that are unknown in the West—for example, **bishi**, "the dying of a beautiful death." Equally, one hope for beleaguered western corporations is that Japan's mighty manufacturing industry may ultimately be brought down "by its own internal contradictions" for, while we may regard briskness, decisiveness, and force of character as qualities appropriate, even essential, to a business leader, in Japan a *leader* must cultivate *indecisiveness*, and a *rabble-rousing presenter* will be highly regarded for his *nimble pussy-footing around the subject*. At Japanese meetings we are always reminded of Churchill's celebrated attack on the Labour prime minister as "Decided only to be undecided, resolved to be irresolute, adamant for drift, solid for fluidity."

Should you wish any proposals you make to stand even a modest chance of making it through the spongy land of mists that is the Japanese meeting, we recommend that you speak slowly (and repetitively) and carry a big... chart! See why, below.

Yes

THE TEN REASONS TO EMPLOY CHARTS

The best way in which to gain control of the drifting, rudderless vessel of the Japanese meeting is to unfurl a chart. We have found ten explanations for the Japanese extreme susceptibility to charts.

• ONE
Japanese education emphasizes rote-learning, and Japanese examinations are invariably in the form of multiple-choice tests, thus even a "high-level" Japanese education is no guarantee whatsoever of the ability to arrange one's thoughts or express them clearly. A chart provides an indispensable mental walking-stick, a stiffening exo-skeleton to the sprawling, invertebrate mind of both the speaker and the spoken to. Moreover, this examination-based education system accustoms people to bite-size pieces of information, consequently the Japanese audience prefers information when it is presented in the ippin-ryori form of a clearly divided flow chart, not in *steak-size lumps of prose*.

• TWO
Those same tests in which the Japanese excel are chiefly mathematical. Consequently they feel more comfortable with even non-numerical information when it is presented in a pseudo-scientific form.

• THREE
Japanese people's weakness for statistics is well-known. How many times has we been told that over 90% of the country consider themselves middle-class (the other 10% are presumably *rentier* rather than proletarian). Thus when making a chart, regardless of the subject, it should be as full of numerical data as possible. *The six reasons to buy this product, The nine factors influencing purchase decisions, The ten reasons to employ charts.*

The chart should be as firm, confident, and over-stated as the meeting itself is diffuse, unfocused, and underplayed. Since Japanese people have misspent their youth memorizing the contents of books with titles such as *The 1000 Most Essential English Expressions to get into the High School of Your Choice*, or *The 36 Maths Questions Most Likely to Come Up in Your Entrance Exam*, they are left with a Pavlovian reverence for such numbers. They have a weakness for the finite and the measurable.

FOUR

As with ikebana, the tea ceremony, judo, and karate, the Japanese tend to believe there is *a correct way to do everything*, a certain road that must be followed. The blocks and arrows of a chart form mental stepping stones of the michi that leads to an inevitable conclusion. Something is credible in proportion as it is methodical and deliberate.

FIVE

Another explanation for chartophilia is the relative decline of literacy. Since the war, school and university class numbers have risen to such levels that, while illiteracy has been eradicated, literacy has *qualitively* declined. This decline has been abetted by the rise of television and *manga* (comic books). It is often noted with regret that instruction booklets for even the simplest machines now come in comic book form. The businessman's fondness for charts is a related phenomenon. Information is moving from the *hard* world of letters to the *soft* world of pictures.

SIX

Preparing for a meeting appears to be one of the few areas of life in Japan in which the old world ideal of the *gentleman amateur*, doing things negligently but with redeeming panache, still obtains. You can bet that any documentation you have carefully provided in advance will only be looked at for the first time in the course of the meeting. What you write must therefore be both sufficiently legible and adequately intelligible that it can be absorbed at the same time as green tea, tobacco smoke, telephone messages, and, of course, the proceedings of the meeting itself.

SEVEN

The Japanese decision-making process is notoriously labyrinthine. Your charts will inevitably be carried off to persuade sundry *eminences grises* (kuromaku, or black curtains) whose approval is necessary before any progress can be made in your suit. Thus, when you are making materials to support your own presentation, you must bear in mind that you are also providing the text for a number of sub-presentations, probably more important than your own. It is prudent then to provide all the necessary information in a highly portable and intelligible form, so that the downstream users need only insert a few conjunctions for the thing to come alive.

EIGHT

Surprisingly for a technophiliac nation, computer-created charts still have the power to fill the Japanese kachō, buchō, or shachō with reverence and awe. Those in the upper ranks tend to be middle-aged computer illiterates, quite unversed in even preinstalled graphics software.

NINE

One peculiar characteristic of the Japanese businessman is his extraordinary knack of entirely missing the thrust of a presentation and instead, focusing insistently on some totally irrelevant and insignificant point. It is not clear whether this is a sophisticated negotiating technique, the expression of an antisocial impulse, some species of modern day *zenmondo*, or just the consequence of extreme mental pedestrianism. To give an example, if one were pitching to run an ad-campaign for a new brand of TV, it might be as well to include a chart showing the influence of global stars from Charlie Chaplin to Arnold Schwarzenegger on twentieth century tastes in entertainment—*just in case*. We have labelled this the "preemptive strike of redundant information."

TEN

You can win *kudos* and business through charts simply because they are a physical proof of *ganbarism*, of having labored late sustained by fetid shrink-wrapped food. This has led to the birth of a school of chart-mongers who seek to impress by the *size* of their productions rather than by their *quality*. One can see some veritable Bayeux Tapestries (or, to be more appropriately Oriental, Great Walls) of the chart world—charts whose monstrous size is often in direct proportion to their emptiness. A couple of examples of egregious charts I have seen—One purported to explain the relationship between the Vietnam war and the Japanese soft-drink market, another the options available to a "fallen" woman as she approached the end of her shelf-life!

To understand such charts we must return to the middle ages, when knights who had done brave battle in the tourney would present their blood and sweat drenched tunics to fair ladyes as a token of love. The sweat and can-coffee soiled chart seems to be one way to woo business partners in modern Japan. The chart's significance is not in what it says, but in the noble toil implicit in it. Gambarism, after all, must be rewarded.

EXPLANATORY NOTES TO CHART ONE

This chart was produced by Watanabe to give McVitie Consulting's interpretation of long-term trends in the computer market. While the American manager, forced to appease the greed of his stockholders, thinks in terms of quarters, the Japanese manager can think long-term, forward and back. McVitie's subsequent suggestions for revitalizing Suzuki Denki shall all be based on this overview.

If the first chart is judged with extreme charity it could be described as historically perceptive, broad in sweep, grandilo-

OA業界長期的なトレンド		
1900	タイプライター	・女性を男尊女卑の束縛から解放 ・効率的であっても機能的なだけ ・個性を発揮する機会にならなかった
1950	メーンフレーム	・巨大組織、政府のためのもの ・メーカーも独占企業 ・技術者でないと絶対使えない、堅く使い難いイメージ ・コストも高い、サイズも大きい ・Organization man つまり50年代の個性を発揮しようと思わないアメリカ人のサラリーマンにピッタシ ・冷戦時代にあてはまるもの
1980	ワープロ	・機能がグレードアップされたタイプライターに過ぎない ・デザイン、カラーはまだまだ ・地味な事務所くさいイメージからまだ脱皮していない
	パソコン	・最初から反体制的な味が強い ・独占企業への元気なチャレンジ ・一般の人が理解できるほど使いやすい、買うことができるほど安い定価という個人を優先にするヒッピーっぽい価値感 ・自分なりに自分の個性を発揮できる ・地味ではないイメージがキーポイント
1990 激変期	ネットワーク ↓ ?	秘密主義 → オープン化　日本中心主義 → 世界主義　大量生産 → オーダーメイド　一貫生産 → 外部調達　製品 → マーケティング INDIVIDUAL CREATIVE MIND

quent, questioning and inspiring. If, however, we judge it sincerely we are forced to denounce it as cliché-ridden, general to the point of meaninglessness, open-ended and concluding with gibberish English.

As we stated in the introduction, Japanese businessmen like charts. They like the whole flow of history to culminate in their product. They love generalizations, dubious logic, and most of all incorrect, but high-sounding, English. This chart is thus a perfect specimen of Nipponese chart fetishism.

LONG TERM TRENDS IN OFFICE AUTOMATION

1900's	TYPEWRITER	• Released women from bondage of male chauvinism • Increased efficiency, however ultimately was merely functional • Did not provide opportunity for expression of individuality
1950's	MAINFRAME	• Serves giant organizations/governments • Manufacturer is a monopoly producer • Only comprehensible to engineers • Product has hard, user-unfriendly image • High cost and large size • Matches perfectly the needs of 'Organization Man'—the unambitious employee of 1950s big business America • Suitable for the cold war era
1980's	WORD-PROCESSOR	• Ultimately is little more than a superior typewriter • Desk Top Publishing, Color functions inadequate • Fails to cast off dreary, gray 'office' image

	PERSONAL COMPUTER	• From day one had a strong, anti-establishment image
		• Prepared to take on giant, monopoly business
		• Individualistic hippy mentality
		  Easy enough for the non-specialist to use
		  Cheap enough for the average consumer to buy
		• Provides opportunities for self-expression
		• Stylish, cool image is crucial

1990's DRAMATIC CHANGE	NETWORK COMPUTER ?	(SECRECY) (JAPANO-CENTRISM) (MASS-PRODUCTION) (INTEGRATED PRODUCTION) (PRODUCT-FOCUSED) (OPENNESS) (CUSTOMIZATION) (MARKETING) (GLOBALISM) (OUT-SOURCING)

EMPOWERMENT OF THE INDIVIDUAL

Brand Senryaku
Presentation

Watanabe: Wareware ga kangaeta atarashii **maaketingu [marketing] senryaku** o setsumei suru mae ni, chotto **waapuro [**word-pro**cessor] gyōkai no chōkiteki-na nagare** o mite mitai to omoimasu.

Chuck: Jūkyū-seiki no owari gurai ni tanjō shita **taipuraitaa [typewriter]** kara hajimaru mono desu...

Watanabe: Taipuraitaa [typewriter] ga shakai ni dono yō na kōka o motarashita ka o kangaeru to, **dansonjohi ni yotte, yoi shokuba kara shatto-auto [shut out] sareta ita josei ni, iroiro-na michi o hiraita.** Tsumari, **kaihōsha no yō na mono deshita.**

Chuck: Gyaku ni, tsugi ni deta **meenfureemu [mainframe]** wa kojin no tachiba de wa naku, **kyodaina soshiki o kyōka suru kōka** ga attan' desu.

Watanabe: Sono go, yori kibo no chiisai, kakaku no hikui waapuro [word-pro**cessor] ga dete, shigoto o yori kantan ni shimashita ga, shigoto o tanoshiku, koseiteki-ni suru ni wa itarimasen deshita. Sore wa pasokon [perso**nal-com**puter] ga tassei shita koto da, to iemasu. **PC o meguru kiiwaado [keyword] wa, tsukai-yasui, tanoshii, kurieitibu [creative], kakumeiteki, tsumari PC wa kojin ga soshiki ni katsu buki na wake desu.**

Chuck: Hitokoto de ieba, **kurōzu [close] kara ōpun [open] e no shifuto [shift]**.

Watanabe: Chaato [chart] o goran ni natte kudasai. **Samazama-na shifuto [shift]** o risuto-appu [list-up] shite arimasu. **Soshiki** kara **kojin, Nihon-chūshin-shugi** kara **gurōbaru-maindo [global mind], himitsu-shugi** kara **nettowaaku [net-work], shanai-ikkan-seisan** kara **gaibu-chōtatsu** to **chūkaku-nōryoku, seizō** kara **maaketingu [marketing]** e—kono yō na koto o beesu [base] ni shite, wareware wa "**creative individual mind**" to iu teema [theme] ni shitagatta kaisha no fukkatsusaku o kangaete orimasu.

Chuck: Sō iu yō na koto o kirikuchi ni shite, **burando [brand]-senryaku** no hanashi ni hairimashō.

ブランド戦略プレゼンテーション

In this presentation, Chuck and Watanabe talk the employees of Suzuki Denki through the first chart which gives McVitie Consulting's interpretation of the history of typewriters, word-processors, and computers. Chuck and Watanabe aim to persuade their audience that the key trend is a shift from joyless functional technology serving the giant organization to technology that empowers the individual.

ワタナベ： 我々が考えた新しいマーケティング戦略を説明する前に、ちょっとワープロ業界の長期的な流れを見てみたいと思います。

チャック： 19世紀の終りぐらいに誕生したタイプライターから始まるものです…。

ワタナベ： タイプライターが社会にどのような効果をもたらしたかを考えると、男尊女卑によって、良い職場からシャットアウトされていた女性に、いろいろな道を開いた。つまり、解放者のようなものでした。

チャック： 逆に、次に出たメーンフレームは個人の立場ではなく、巨大な組織を強化する効果があったんです。

ワタナベ： その後、より規模の小さい、価格の低いワープロが出て、仕事をより簡単にしましたが、仕事を楽しく、個性的にするにはいたりませんでした。それはパソコンが達成したことだ、と言えます。PCをめぐるキーワードは、使いやすい、楽しい、クリエイティブ、革命的、つまりPCは個人が組織に勝つ武器なわけです。

チャック： 一言で言えば、クローズからオープンへのシフト。

Brand Strategy Presentation

チャックさんと渡部さんは、鈴木電気での第一回目のプレゼンテーションをしています。はじめにチャートをもとに、タイプライターから現在のPCへの移行の概略と社会への影響を説明し、鈴木電気再生のためのテーマを定義しています。

Watanabe: Before explaining the new **marketing strategy** that we have devised, we'd like first to consider **long-term trends in the word-processor business**.

Chuck: It starts around the end of the nineteenth century with the birth of the **typewriter**.

Watanabe: If we consider what effects the typewriter had on society, we can see that it **opened up various possibilities to women until then excluded from good jobs through male chauvinism**. In short it was **a kind of liberator**.

Chuck: On the other hand, the mainframe computer which came out next did not have the effect of empowering the individual, but rather **making still more powerful the giant organization**.

Watanabe: After that the cheaper and smaller **word processor** came out which, although it made work simpler, did not make it more fun or more individualistic. You can say that that was achieved by the **PC**. **In the case of the PC, the keywords are user-friendly, fun, creative, revolutionary—In short the PC is a weapon that enables the little man to beat the big organization**.

Chuck: Basically it's **a shift from closedness to openness**…

ワタナベ： チャートをご覧になって下さい。さまざまなシフトをリスト・アップしてあります。組織から個人、日本中心主義からグローバル・マインド、秘密主義からネットワーク、社内一貫生産から外部調達と中核能力へ、製造からマーケッティングへ：このようなことをベースにして、我々は CREATIVE INDIVIDUAL MIND というテーマにしたがった会社の復活策を考えております。

チャック： そういうようなことを切り口にして、今後のブランド戦略の話に入りましょう。

Watanabe: If you look at the chart you can see that we've listed some of the major shifts taking place at the moment—from **the organization to the individual, from Japanocentrism to globalism, from secrecy to networks, from integrated vertical production to outsourcing and core competencies, from production to marketing**—starting from these insights, we've developed a strategy to revive your company based on the concept of "the empowerment of the individual.".

Chuck: So, using these ideas as a spring board, I'd like to begin talking about **brand strategy**.

Know-it-all Notes

• Typewriter　タイプライター

The typewriter was actually invented in 1714. Since, however, elegant handwriting was a sign of social class, it took a long time for the machine to take off commercially. This timelag between an invention being made and it really shaking things up is a phenomenon observed in the case of cars, television etc. of which the commercial potential was only fully realized decades after the technology had been created.

• Kyodai-na soshiki　巨大な組織

Given the colossal size of many major Japanese companies, the whole question of retaining dynamism in a large organization is a big theme in Japan. Note the terms Daikigyōbyō (Big Business Disease), and Eikokubyō, the English disease, or apathy-induced long-term economic decline.

• Kakaku　価格

Price. The word nedan is slightly less formal, and thus less appropriate to a business meeting. Note the compound word Kakakuhakai—*price destruction*, used to describe the discount boom provoked by the Japanese consumer's post-1991 quest for value for money (maxvalue). Also note kakaku only refers to the price of goods, ryōkin is used for services.

There is a proverb in Japan Yasukarō, warukarō (if it's cheap, it's nasty), and until the bursting of the bubble the Japanese were almost pathological devotees of absurdly over-priced branded goods. Tea had to be *Fortnums* or *Fauchon*, wine had to be from France, not from closer and cheaper sources like California or Australia. This brand fetish is visible even in the most simple accessories. Check out the *Givenchy* belts and *Playboy* or *Arnold Palmer* socks of your salaryman counterparts!

• Keyword　キーワード

The Japanese adore the concept of the keyword which is not regarded as at all gimmicky. We strongly recommend using keyword-lists at least once in every presentation.

• Tairyō-seisan/OrderMade　大量生産／オーダーメイド

Examples of success with customization in the field of personal computers would be Dell Computer and Gateway 2000 (see Chapter 10).

• Shanai-ikkan-seisan　社内一貫生産

Vertically-integrated production. Even if large Japanese companies do not produce everything they need for the final product in-house, they frequently forbid their sub-contractors from producing for anyone else. In return they will not look for alternative (and probably cheaper) sources of supply, and will continue to place orders even in a recession. Fujitsu, however, bucked the trend and doubled their share of the PC market in 1995-96 by boldly moving to out-sourcing (gaibu-chōtatsu) from low-cost foreign manufactures.

• Seizō　製造

Production. The industrial sector is called seizōgyō. The world of finance the kin'yūkai. The Japanese, with their reverence for manufacture, regard only the former as the jitsukeizai—the *real* economy. An example of a company that achieved great success by emphasis on clever marketing would be Acer with its Aspire range of well-designed, colored home computers, or Apple, which had great success by targeting schools and colleges.

• CREATIVE INDIVIDUAL MIND

What does this mean? Very probably nothing. At moments of extreme excitement Japanese businessmen like to speak with the oracular profundity and obscurity that katakana can so conveniently provide. The slogan or theme phrase need not be meaningful *per se*, because it will be endowed with meaning by its use as a war-cry and a rallying-point.

• Kirikuchi ni shite　切り口にして

A classic business Japanese phrase, meaning something like *using as a springboard*, or *approaching from this angle*.

物知り英語ノート

- **Before explaining XX, we'd like first to...**

ミーティングやプレゼンテーションの時、本題に入る前に大まかにその目的などを説明するための表現です。次のような表現も覚えておくと便利です。

> We'd like to give an <u>overview</u> of XXX（概観）
> We'd like to give a brief <u>outline</u> of XXX（概略）
> We'd like to briefly <u>run through</u> XXX（目を通す）

- **Chauvinism**

"ショービニズム、排他（優越）主義" 男尊女卑にあう表現は英語にはありませんが、一番近いと思われるのは **Male chauvinism**（男性優越主義）といえます。

- **On the other hand**

"逆に" 他の言い方として **By contrast** がります。

- **Empower**

"強くする、力を与える" 現在、アメリカでキーワードとなっている単語です。社会で弱い存在である女性、マイノリティ、そして組織に対する個人に権限が与えられることで、かれらは夢を実現させる可能性を見い出しました。

- **Still more powerful**

この **Still** は「まだ」という意味ではありません。ここでは **More** を強める副詞として使われ、今までも力があったものがますます力を強めているというように使われています。**Yet more powerful** のように **yet** も同じように使われます。

- **Little man**

"一般の人、平凡な人"

- **Strategic ideas**

ここで渡部さんは、国際市場へ参入するためのマーケティング戦略をか

いつまんで下記のように説明しています。まずアウトソーシングで安い部品を調達し、ネットワークに対応できるオープンシフトの商品を製造すること。そして商品を国際市場で印象的な宣伝を通してマーケティングし、ひとりひとりにアピールできる個性のあるものにしなければばらない。

• Using these ideas as a springboard

springboard の直訳は跳躍台のことで、ここでは"出発点"を意味しています。同じような意味で次の表現も使うことができます。**Basing our discussion loosely on these ideas.／Using these ideas as a starting point.**

EXPLANATORY NOTES TO CHART TWO

This chart is far less high-faluting than the first. Watanabe and Chuck have decided to replace the Sumo brand word-processor with a new brand of cutting-edge Internet PC. The technology is simple, but marketing holds the key to success. The consultants therefore regard the new name as all important. What are the key points that the name should communicate? Chuck and Watanabe review their competitors' product names by dividing them and their supporting slogans into four broad categories and analyzing them, before producing their new name and slogan at the bottom of the chart.

パソコン業界のネーミング／スローガン分析チャート

科学的タイプ	パワーを感じさせるタイプ
NEWTON	POWERBOOK
ZAURUS	CANBE
MEBIUS	DYNABOOK
THINKPAD	PRONOTE
BIBLO	DESKPOWER
	WINBOOK

名前

キーワード

哲学的なイメージのラテン語／ギリシャ語的な接尾語	情報処理速度 可能性を追及 成功／プロ

合理的なアピール ▶ ▶

Where do you want to go today? . Has it changed your life yet?	Solutions for a small planet The network is the computer

スローガン

可能性を追及	ネットワーク

キーワード

ATARASHII NAME

ネーミング・ベネフィット

可能性、夢
ネットワーク、インターネットをイメージ
周辺機器へのネーミング展開が可能

楽しいタイプ	音でアピールする タイプ
APPLE WOODY RUPO PACK-MATE	APTIVA PRAESARIO PROLINEA CONTURA BREZZA FLORA

楽しさ 使いやすさ ユーザーフレンドリー	格好の良さ デザイン ライフスタイル

▶ ▶ 非合理的なアピール

Your trusted adviser You've got a friend in the business	Intel Inside

信頼性	ブランド名を強化

キーワード

ATARASHII SLOGAN

スローガン・ベネフィット

可能性と明日への夢や希望をイメージさせる
ネーミングとスローガンの相乗効果

Analysis of PC product names & slogans

NAMES

SCIENTIFIC TYPE	POWER TYPE
NEWTON	POWERBOOK
ZAURUS	CANBE
MEBIUS	DYNABOOK
THINKPAD	PRONOTE
BIBLO	DESKPOWER
	WINBOOK

Philosphical Image Latin / Greek endings	High Speed Fulfilment of Potential Professionalism

RATIONAL APPEAL

SLOGANS

Where do you want to go today? Has it changed your life yet?	Solutions for a small planet The network is the computer

SELF–FULFILMENT	NETWORK

NEW NAME

DREAM TEAM

Emphasizes fulfilling potential
Suggests Networks / The Internet
Can be extended to peripherals

FUN TYPE	**SOUND TYPE**
APPLE	APTIVA
WOODY	PRAESARIO
RUPO	PROLINEA
PACK-MATE	CONTURA
	BREZZA
	FLORA

Fun	Cool & Fashionable
Easy to use	Design
User-friendly	Lifestyle

▶ ▶ IRRATIONAL APPEAL

Your trusted adviser	Intel Inside
You've got a friend in the business	

RELIABILITY   REINFORCE · BRAND NAME

NEW SLOGAN

Your dreams come true:
Positive associations
Slogan and name are mutually reinforcing

Shin-Naming to Slogan no Presentation

Chuck: Mazu saisho ni, **sude ni shijō ni dete iru shōhin no neemingu [naming]** ni me o tooshitai to omoimasu.

Watanabe: Neemingu [naming] o bunrui suru to, kihonte-ki ni yottsu no omona taipu [type] ga arimasu. Sono yottsu no tokuchō o kantan ni bunseki suru to, hitotsume wa **kagaku-tekina neemingu [naming]**, futatsume wa **pawaa [power] o kan-jisaseru neemingu [naming]**, tsugi wa **tanoshisa o kyōchō suru neemingu**, soshite saigo ni, **oto no hibiki o jūshi suru neemingu [naming]**. Maa, daitai kono yō na mono desu. Kono **yottsu no neemingu [naming] no kiiteema [key theme]** o pikku-appu [pick up] suru to, hidari kara migi e mukatte, **chishiki, chisei**, soshite **johō-shori-sokudo, puro [professional] de aru koto**, sono tsugi wa iwayuru **yūzaa-furendorii [user-friendly]** de aru koto. Saigo ni, **kakkō yosa, ryūkōsei**, tsumari **PC wa wakamono ni fukaketsu-na akusesarii [accessory]** toshite apiiru [appeal] suru to iu kangae desu.

Chuck: Neemingu [naming] kara **surogan [slogan]** e me o mukeru to, kigyō wa surogan [slogan] o tooshite dono yō na messeji [message] o tsu-taete iru deshō ka.

Watanabe: Wareware no kenkyū ni yoru to, **yottsu no pataan [pattern]** ga aru to omoimasu. Sore wa mazu **potensharu [potential] o tsuikyū dekiru to iu mono**, soshite, **jisedai PC**, tsumari **nettowaaku [network] o kyōchō suru mono**, sorekara **burando [brand]-mei o tsuyomeru taipu [type]**, soshite saigo ni **shinraisei o apiiru [appeal] suru mono** nado desu.

Chuck: Kono yō na teema [theme] o ishiki shinagara, wareware wa **onsha no shin-imeeji [image]** o kaihatsu shite kimashita.

Watanabe: Soshite **Dreamteam *Your dreams come true* to iu shōhinmei o tsukuri-agemashita.**

Chuck: Saishūteki ni ikutsu ka no an kara naze kore o eranda ka to iu to, **TEAM** to iu kotoba o tsukau to **genki-de dainamiku [dynamic]-na imeeji [image] ga tsuyoku, kanrenkiki ni mo kakudai dekiru**. Namae ga Eigo ni natte iru koto ni wa **kaigai de mo tsūyō shi**, kokunai de wa Nihonmei yori imeeji [image] ga **furukusakunaku, modan [modern] de Amerika-teki** to iu benefitto [benefit] ga arimasu.

新ネーミングとスローガンのプレゼンテーション

Here Watanabe and Chuck go on to the second chart, first reviewing the brandnames used by the leading PC manufacturers in the US and Japan, then considering what kind of slogans are being used to reinforce brand identity in the PC marketplace. Based on their analysis of key themes they propose a new name and slogan to replace Suzuki Denki's long-standing SUMO word-processor brandname, the rather parochial and outdated brainchild of Tomita.

チャック： まず最初に、すでに市場に出ている商品のネーミングに目を通したいと思います。

ワタナベ： ネーミングを分類すると、基本的に四つの主なタイプがあります。その四つの特徴を簡単に分析すると、一つ目は科学的なネーミング、二つ目はパワーを感じさせるネーミング、次は楽しさを強調するネーミング、そして最後に、音のひびきを重視するネーミング。まあ、大体このようなものです。この四つのネーミングのキーテーマをピックアップすると、左から右へ向かって、**知識、知性、そして情報処理速度、プロであること、その次はいわゆるユーザーフレンドリーであること。最後に、格好良さ、流行性、つまり PC は若者に不可欠なアクセサリーとしてアピールするという考えです。**

チャック： ネーミングからスローガンへ目を向けると、企業はスローガンを通してどのようなメッセージを伝えているでしょうか。

Naming Presentation

鈴木電気を再生させるためにはPC市場への参入が不可欠です。そのためには既存のブランド名「相撲」を捨て、世界に通用するネーミングが必要であることを説得したいチャックさんと渡部さんは、日本国内およびアメリカのPC市場に出ているネーミング及びスローガンについての分析、解説をそれぞれ4つに分類し、チャートを使いながら行っています。その後、鈴木電気のために開発した新商品名を提案し解説しています。

Chuck: Well, first of all we'd like to take a quick look at **the names of products already on the market**.

Watanabe: If we break up the names into groups, there are basically four main types. If we make a simple analysis of the characteristics of the four groups, the first group is **scientific names**, the second, **names that have a feel of power**, then **product names that emphasize enjoyment**, and finally **names which regard a good sound as most important**. Yes, that's more or less the picture. If we now just have look at the **key themes of these different name types**, we get, from left to right, **knowledge and intelligence**, then **speed of information processing and professionalism**, then next comes what's called **user-friendliness**. Finally, we get **cool, fashion**—basically the idea of appealing to consumers by presenting the PC as **an indispensable accessory for young people**.

Chuck: If we now switch out attention from names to **slogans**... What kind of message are companies trying to get across through their slogans?

ワタナベ： 我々の研究によると、四つのパターンがあると思います。それはまずポテンシャルを追及出来るというもの、そして次世代PCつまりネットワークを強調するもの、それからフランド名を強めているタイプ、最後に信頼性をアピールするものなどです。

チャック： このようなテーマを意識しながら、我々は御社の新イメージを開発してきました。

ワタナベ： そして Dreamteam: Your dreams come true という商品名を作り上げました。

チャック： 最終的にいくつかの案からなぜこれを選んだかというと、TEAM と言う言葉を使うと元気でダイナミクな印象が強く、関連機器にも拡大できる。名前が英語になっていることには、海外でも通用し、国内では日本名よりイメージが古くさくなく、モダンでアメリカ的というベネフィットがあります。

Watanabe: Well, according to our research, there are **four patterns**. These are respectively to be able to **fulfil your potential**, to **emphasize next-generation computing—in other words, the network—**then there's **the kind that reinforces the brand name**, and finally **the type that makes reliability its point of appeal**.

Watanabe: So, keeping all these various themes in mind, we went about **developing your new brand image**…

Chuck: And we came up with the **new name Dreamteam:** *Your dreams come true*.

Watanabe: Finally, let me explain why we chose this name out of a large number of candidates. The word Team gives a **strong impression of energy and dynamism**, while it can also be **extended to peripherals**. The benefits of having an English name are that it **can be used abroad**, while within Japan it has **a less stuffy image** than a Japanese name, in short, **it sounds modern and American**!

Know-it-all Notes

• Mazu saisho ni　まず最初に

Well, first of all. Other handy opening phrase are **sate** (let's get down to business) and **sore de**, meaning something like *Right then*, or *so then*....

• Ni me o tooshitai　に目を通したい

Lit: To run my eye over, but better translated *to review briefly, to run through*. Since the Japanese are not made to write essays at school, they are often surprisingly bad at marshalling their thoughts. As any one who has had the misfortune to attend a Japanese wedding will know, speech-making is definitely not an area in which Japan is number one. You can therefore make a long, tedious and rambling speech without fear of boring your audience. They expect to be bored anyway!

• Naming　ネーミング

This is an area taken very seriously in Japan, where certain names that appeal to the Japanese prove a disaster when exported abroad. While Walkman, for all it's being incorrect English was a huge PR success in foreign markets, Pocari Sweat, the health drink, is, for obvious reasons, marketed merely as Pocari abroad.

Obviously Chuck and Watanabe feel that Sumo is an excessively Japanese name for a product that is to be launched in the global market, and that while names like Shogun, Samurai, or Ninja might do for cars or motorbikes, a computer needs a less traditional name suggestive of more than just brute force.

• Hitotsume　一つ目

Note how Watanabe varies the list here with **hitotsume, futatsume, tsugi wa, soshite saigo-ni**. Learning how to reel off lists is an essential part of business speaking.

• Kyōchō suru   強調する

To emphasize. In this case interchangeable with jūshi suru (to regard as important).

• Daitai kono yō na mono desu   大体このようなものです

That's pretty much the situation. A useful, if slightly casual, phrase for summing up.

• Chishiki/Chisei   知識／知性

The former means knowledge, the latter wit or cleverness.

• Pro de aru koto   プロであること

Note how in a business presentation the slightly pompous de aru is used for *to be.*

• Iwayuru   いわゆる

Equivalent to something like "what is generally called..."

• Me o mukeru   目を向ける

A useful transitional phrase. *If we now turn our attention to...*

• Jisedai PC   次世代PC

When talking of the future, jisedai (next generation) is a strong competitor to 21-seiki!

• Ishiki shinagara   意識しながら

Bearing such themes in mind. A useful high-sounding phrase.

• Dreams come true   ドリームカムツルー

There is a pop group in Japan of this name, so thanks to them the slogan achieves instant memorability. A cynical explanation for the Japanese addiction to the theme of "dream" is that it's the consequence of the extremely low quality of life. In your tiny apartment, on the crowded trains, in the open-plan office, during one's meager holidays, the most you can hope for yourself is to be able to cherish an unrealizable dream, to have a private and inviolable fantasy. Signs of this tendency to flee from, or just ignore reality (Genjitsu-tōhi) are the rather anachronistic fondness for heavily blurred photographs, the love of Disneyland and other theme parks—that Europeans, at least, regard as merely childish—and wildly extravagant and theatrical weddings (hadekon).

• Tsukuri-agemashita   作り上げました

The use of a compound verb makes the process of creating the name seem more laborious. See the section on compound verbs in Chapter 8.

• Kanrenkiki   関連機器

Peripherals—printers, scanners, digital cameras. An example of this kind of brand family would be Epson's Colorio, a name used for printers, scanners, and digital cameras. Ricoh used to apply the prefix Ri- to its products (Ricopy, Ricut). Moving to the foods sector Nestlé reinforces recollection by repetition of the prefix Nes-, as in Nescafé, Nestea, and Nesquik.

• Eigo   英語

Although the Japanese tend to regard foreign *products* with suspicion, they definitely prefer foreign names for domestic products since they feel more modern.

物知り英語ノート

• **First of all**
"まず最初に"

• **Take a quick look**
欧米でのプレゼンテーションでは簡潔性が重視されます。ここでは **Quick** という単語を使い「素早く」という以外に効率的にというニュアンスを含めています。

• **Break up the names into groups**
"グループに分ける" という意味で、正しくは **classify**（分類化する）といいますが、**Break up...** の方が力強さを感じさせます。このように、ビジネスの時には口語を選んだほうが聞き手にインパクトを与えることができます。科学的な言葉とパワフルな言葉をバランスよく使い分けることも大切です。

• **The first / the second / then / and finally**
第1から始まってポイントを手際よく並べ、プレゼンを進めていくことが大切です。

• **That's more or less the picture**
picture は "現状、状況" という意味で使われています。同じように **That's pretty much the state of things** を使うこともできます。

• **...basically**
"結局、何かというと"。説明的な役割を果たします。

• **If we now switch our attention**
新しい話題に入る時に使われます。**If** はお伺いをたてているようなニュアンスをもっています。**If we now turn to／move on to** も同じように使われます。

• In other words… the network

"つまり（いわゆる）、ネットワーク" 前に挙げたものを説明する時に使われます。

例：He's indecisive, in other words a typical salaryman
　　「彼は優柔不断です。つまり典型的なサラリーマンです」

• Keeping all these different themes in mind

"これらのテーマを<u>意識しながら</u>" 覚えておくと役立つ表現です。

• The name

日本人は「夢」「未来」「希望」などの言葉を好んでスローガンやネーミングに取り入れる傾向があります。鈴木電気に提案した **Dream Team** などは、夢に向かって皆でがんばろうというようなイメージで特に日本人好みではないでしょうか。また、**Team** を使っているのでコンピュータ周辺機器への **Brand Extension**（新製品や改良品を市場に出す時に、すでに成功しているブランド名を使用すること。例：コカコーラのチェリーコーク／ダイエットコーク）の際にも有利です。

• English name

Compaq、**Apple**、**IBM**、**HP** のようなアメリカの多国籍企業が市場を支配している現在、製造国が東南アジアであっても技術はアメリカで生まれたものであることから、ネーミングは英語で行うほうが効果的です。

• A stuffy image

"古くさいイメージ"。**A stuffy person** 頭が硬い、おもしろくない人。

SIX

•

LOCKER-ROOM LANGUAGE & BARRACK-ROOM BANTER

はめをはずすときの会話／試合後の本音

The *civil* and *diffident* Englishmen, the *overbearing* and *pedantic* German, the *epicurean* and *adulterous* Frenchman, the *naïve* and *boisterous* American—according to national stereotypes the Japanese would doubtless find themselves characterized as *obscenely hard-working* and *excruciatingly polite*. For much of the world after all, they remain no more than an obedient Burberry-clad line (the thin beige line) filing down from tour buses, bowing and smiling as they make their purchases and take their photographs. Even for those foreigners who have Japanese friends, their most lasting memory is probably a feeling of shame as they found themselves losing resoundingly in the "battle of the gifts"—that microcosm of the trade war.

With a sigh we must wheel out that old pair of chestnuts, **tatemae** (the mask of propriety) and **honne** (the face beneath the mask). All that the average outsider will be permitted to see or hear of Japanese emotions, goes the conventional wisdom, is the soothing and serene **tatemae** but, nonetheless, underneath writhes the **honne**, the real emotions which are all the stronger and more dangerous for being repressed...

Tatemae and **honne** usually crop up in the negative context of Japanese trade-negotiators being presented as masters of deception, bowing and scraping with infuriating civility as they run another American industry into the ground. We, however, are philologists with no ax to grind, and if we pursue our metaphor further we can see that, once the blank, formal mask is removed and the face revealed *warts and all*, what we are going to see (for all its ugliness!) is something far more expressive, more mobile, and more interesting.

In the office, what with all-night work-frenzies, deadlines to meet, cranky clients to humor and toady up to, the denial of the right to speak one's mind frankly would be too cruel, even for the **gaman**-loving Japanese. Consequently the salaryman enjoys quite an earthy and expressive vocabulary with which to express the highs and lows of his life of toil, tears, and triumph. The language introduced in this chapter is the sincere language of passion, not just bad passions, but also victory and excitement.

Why should you want to use less than polite language with clients?

When speaking to clients language should follow a trough pattern. You will be rigidly formal at the beginning and end of the meeting, but when you get down to the nitty-gritty, a sudden dash of vulgar language can be very persuasive. This is the linguistic equivalent of the cops' tough guy/nice guy routine. First flatter your client, butter him up with sweet nothings, then when he's in your hand tell him good and proper, let him know that if he doesn't buy your product or follow your suggestions he's *really going to be up shit creek!* Abrupt changes in tone are an ancient and highly effective rhetorical trick.

Why should you want to use less than polite language with colleagues?

There are buzzwords for the presentation and for the meeting room, but equally there are buzzwords for the nervous hours before, and the elation after, the event. *Did you kick butt, or did you get your butt kicked?* When winding up or winding down formality is simply unnatural. To be an insider, be one of the boys (regardless of sex), to recount, viking-like, the saga of your deeds, and to contribute to the collective delusion that office-life is a thrilling, manly drama, you must master Japanese locker-room language and barrack-room banter.

We have divided these earthy expressions into two appropriately simple categories: Those that are **1. negative, for insulting, or for playing the gadfly to your colleagues and your clients,** then those that are **2. positive, for praising yourself or, in moments of altruism, your colleagues.**

1. BEING NEGATIVE
ネガティブに話すとき

● 日本に比べて、欧米のサービスはほんとに
　　低レベルのものだ。

Nihon ni kurabete, Ōbei no saabisu [service] wa honto ni **tei-reberu [level]** no mono da.

Compared to Japan, Western service is **at a pretty low level**.

● そんな値段では無理ですよ。話にもならない。

Sonna nedan de wa muri desu yo. **Hanashi ni mo naranai**.

At that price it's impossible! It's just **totally
out of the question**.

● パソコンの時代になってから、ワープロで作った資料は
　　なんかだらしないものに見える。

Pasokon [*personal computer*] no jidai ni natte kara,
waapuro [*word-processor*] de tsukutta shiryō wa
nanka **darashinai** mono ni mieru.

Since PCs came along, documents made on word-processors
somehow look rather **cheap & cheesy**.

● あの不動産開発業者の経理はデタラメだ！

Ano fudōsan-kaihatsu-gyōsha no keiri wa **detarame** da!

That property developer's accounts are just **phoney**!

● クライアントサイドが名門企業だから、仕事を
　　信じられないほど安い金額で受けている。
　　　　評判になるからさあ…

Kurainto-saido [Client-side] ga meimon-kigyō da kara,
shigoto o **shinjirarenai hodo** yasui kingaku de ukete iru.
Hyōban ni naru kara saa…

Since our client is top in his field, we're prepared to do jobs
for them for **unbelievably** small fees. It's good for our
reputation, you see…

● 価格破壊の中で、会社としてやっていくのは
なかなかしんどい。

Kakakuhakai no naka de kaisha toshite yatte iku no wa
nakanaka shindoi.

It's really difficult for the company to keep going with this
level of deflationary pressure (*lit: price destruction*).

● 代理店の連中が言ったことはうさんくさい。マーケ
ティングが商品自体より大切だなんて！

Dairiten no **renchū** ga itta koto wa **usankusai**. Maaketingu
[marketing] ga shōhin-jitai yori taisetsu da nante!

I thought that what the **bunch** of ad-men said was **pretty
dubious**. Marketing is more important than the product
itself—*oh yeah!*

● 新しい戦略をすごくゆっくり説明しないと
向こうはついて来れない。

Atarashii senryaku o sugoku yukkuri setsumei shinai to
mukō wa **tsuite korenai**.

If you don't explain your new strategy incredibly slowly, **the
client** just **won't be able to follow**.

● あの人に期待しないほうがいいよ。他人の顔色しか
窺ってないんだから。

Ano hito ni **kitai shinai** hō ga ii yo. **Tanin no kaoiro shika
ukagatte nain** dakara.

Don't expect much from that guy. He just **adapts himself
to other people's opinions**.

● アメリカの親会社からフォーチュン誌に載った社長が
　日本に来て、怠け者の外人社長の尻に火がついた。

Amerika no oyagaisha kara Fōchun [Fortune]-shi ni notta
kaichō ga Nihon ni kite, namakemono no gaijin-shachō
no **shiri ni hi ga tsuita**.

When the president of the American parent company (who
had been in *Fortune* magazine) came to Japan, it was like
the lazy gaijin boss **had a firecracker up his arse**.

● あの営業マンは口先だけだよ。彼が始める
　プロジェクトはぜったい実現しない。

Ano eigyōman wa **kuchisaki** dake da yo. Kare ga hajimeru
purojekuto [project] wa zettai jitsugen shinai.

That salesman **just talks big**. None of the projects he starts are
ever finished.

2. BEING POSITIVE
ポジティブに話すとき

● 今日はうなるほどおいしい宣伝戦略をもってきました。

Kyō wa **unaru hodo oishii** senden-senryaku o motte
kimashita.

Today I've brought a marketing plan so **exquisite** that it'll set
you **moaning and a-groaning**.

● 業界に詳しくないあの経営コサルタントはうまく
   お客さんをゴマカシタ。

Gyōkai ni kuwashikunai ano keiei konsarutanto [consul-
tant] wa umaku okyaku-san o **gomakashita**.

The Management consultant who knew almost nothing
   about the field **bluffed** pretty convincingly.

● グローバル・マインドというコンセプトを導入した時、
   会議室はすごく盛り上がりました。

Gurōbaru-Maindo [Global Mind] to iu konseputo [concept]
   o dōnyū shita toki, kaigishitsu wa sugoku
   mori-agarimashita.

When I introduced the concept of "thinking globally" the tem-
   perature in the meeting-room **really heated up**.

● この大きな契約をとれれば、もう、ボロ儲けの世界だよ！

Kono ookina keiyaku o torereba, mō, **boromōke no sekai** da yo!

If we can get this big contract, **we're talking mega-bucks**!

● 総会が意外とうまくいって、会長が「無事に終わった、
   よかった」と言った。

Sōkai ga igai ni umaku itte, kaichō ga "**buji ni owatta,
   yokatta**" to itta.

After the stockholders' meeting had gone unexpectedly
   smoothly, the president said "**Thank God we got
   through that OK**."

- 忘年会で社長は、**調子に乗って**二時間の
  スピーチをしたよ。

Bōnenkai de shachō wa, **chōshi ni notte**, nijikan no
supiichi [speech] o shita yo.

At the end-of-year party the boss **got carried away** and made
a two hour speech.

- 韓国の支局に行って、皆が休みをとらず週六日
  働いているところを見て、日本人の社長は
  『**やるな**』としか言えなかった。

Kankoku no shikyoku ni itte, mina ga yasumi o torazu shū-
muika hataraite iru tokoro o mite, Nihonjin no shachō wa
"yaru na" to shika ienakatta.

When the Japanese boss visited the Korean branch and saw
everyone working six days a week without taking any
holidays all he could say was "**Wow! You really
go for it, don't you.**"

- 日本でブランド品を輸入販売すれば、ヒダリうちわだよ。

Nihon de burando [brand]-hin o yunyū-hanbai sureba,
hidari uchiwa da yo.

Importing brand goods into Japan, I tell you it's a **pushover**.

7 Prezen-go no jōkigen

Watanabe: Ore wa **boroboro** da yo!

Chuck: Nee! Asa made ano **rippa-na** hyō o tsukutteta darō?

Watanabe: Maa, **buji ni owatte yokatta**.

Chuck: Aa, **mukō** wa **ooyorokobi** datta. Watanabe-san wa **yarite** da na to…

Watanabe: **Kanshoku** de wa, **umaku itta** to omou?

Chuck: Maa, senryaku no bubun, **tsuite korenai** hito ga ookute chotto **shindokatta**…

Watanabe: Sore wa ieru kamoshirenai. Sono ato wa?

Chuck: Neemingu [naming] no hō, mina wa sugoku **kandō** shita yo. Mina ga Watanabe-san no **paafōmansu [performance] ni muchū** datta!

Watanabe: Maa, tashika ni, saigo no tokoro de sugoi **mori-agatta**!

Chuck: Rei no **DreamTeam** to iu neemingu [naming]-an ga **oo-uke** shita rashii!

Watanabe: **Oishii** shōhinmei da kara, tōzen da! Ano namae dake de besutoseraa [bestseller] ni naru koto machigainashi da!

Chuck: Neemu-chenji [name-change] no tame no konsensasu [consensus] o eru no wa korekara no **tsurai tokoro** da ne…

Watanabe: Ano Tomita wa zettai ni **nekku [neck] ni naru** to, iya-na yokan suru…

プレゼン後の上機嫌

Here Watanabe and Chuck, both rather exhausted, are discussing the reaction to their marketing strategy presentation. Did it all go above their audience's heads? Will their suggestions be acted on, or will that preserver of the status quo Tomita contrive to frustrate them? Will the **Dream Team** remain no more than a dream?

ワタナベ： おれはボロボロだよ。

チャック： ねえ！朝まであの立派な表を作ってただろう？

ワタナベ： まあ、無事に終わってよかった。

チャック： ああ、向こうは大喜びだった。渡部さんはやり手だなぁと…。

ワタナベ： 感触では、うまく行ったと思う？

チャック： まあ、戦略の部分はついてこれない人が多くてちょっとしんどかった。

ワタナベ： それは言えるかも知れない。その後は？

チャック： ネーミングのほう、皆はすごく感動してたよ。皆が渡部さんのパーフォーマンスに夢中だった！

ワタナベ： まあ、確かに、最後のところですごい盛り上がった。

チャック： 例の Dream Team と言うネーミング案が大うけしたらしい。

ワタナベ： オイシイ商品名だから、当然だ！あの名前だけでベストセラーになること間違いなしだ。

チャック： ネーム・チェンジのためのコンセンサスを得るのはこれからの辛いところだね…。

ワタナベ： あの富田は絶対にネックになると、いやな予感する…。

Post Presentation High

第一回目のプレゼンテーションに力を注いでいたチャックさんと渡部さんは少々疲れぎみですが、プレゼンテーションの出来ばえにはかなり満足の様子です。しかし、日本の企業が相手なので、この結果が出るのは少し先のようです。

Watanabe: I'm **shattered**!

Chuck: Yeah! Guess you were up all night making those **cool** charts?

Watanabe: Well, **thank goodness everything went smoothly**.

Chuck: Yes, **the client** was **delighted**, they think you're a **real gung-ho superman**...

Watanabe: So, from **the vibes**, do you think it **went well**?

Chuck: Well, the strategy part was **a little hairy** because a lot of people just **couldn't follow**...

Watanabe: I think you're probably right. How about after that?

Chuck: As for the naming bit, they were **orgasmic**. Everyone was **overwhelmed** by your performance!

Watanabe: Well it's certainly true that towards the end things **started to rock and roll**!

Chuck: That **DreamTeam** name idea was **a blockbuster hit**!

Watanabe: There's no doubt it's a **fabulous** name. Make no mistake, their products can become bestsellers thanks to that name alone!

Chuck: The **tough part** now is achieving a consensus about the name change.

Watanabe: Yeah, I've got a bad feeling that Tomita's going to **put a spanner in the works**...

Know-it-all Notes

• Ore おれ

At a presentation Watanabe would use the pronoun watakushi, or speak on behalf of his company (watakushi-domo, wareware, waga-sha). Here, as he is being informal, he uses a shorter, rougher-sounding word for "I." Note that this pronoun can only be used by men.

• Boroboro ボロボロ

An onomatopoeic word, usually used to mean *dilapidated, ragged*. The British English equivalent might be "knackered."

• Nee ねえ

Here this means something like "I know what you mean."

• Hyō 表

Chuck here chooses to use the native Japanese word for *chart*.

• Buji ni owatte, yokatta 無事に終わって、よかった

The Japanese love understatement, and perhaps—like the gloomy Brits who respond to the question "How are you?" with a "Not too bad, I suppose,"—tend to think a good thing equals no more than the absence of a bad thing. A translation might be something like *"No major catastrophes occurred"* or *"Thank God, we got through that OK."*

• Mukō 向こう

Literally meaning "over there," this refers to the people on the other side of the table, the *client*.

• Yarite やり手

Literally "a doing hand," an *achiever*. This word is not uniformly positive in its implications. Yarite-baba (an achieving hag) refers to a middle-aged pimpess, and evokes the less salubrious meaning of yaru (to do *it*).

• Kanshoku　感触

Literally, "texture," an important word in Japanese business. Your counterparts in a meeting may say nothing more explcit than **sō desu ka** (indeed?), or **naruhodo** (of course!), but however bland their words you can probably judge their thoughts by the atmosphere and mood in the room. Try and develop a sixth sense for this!

• Tsuite-korenai　ついてこれない

As the "Banker's Trust tapes scandal" has shown, a degree of contempt for the client is a fact of life in business. Here Chuck is referring to those who couldn't keep up with or follow their rather dubious and sophistic potted history of computers.

• Ieru kamoshirenai　言えるかもしれない

Lit: "It may be possible to say that," this phrase is better rendered as "You *may* be right/You *may* have a point there." A typically uncommitted, fence-sitting, diffident expression.

• Kandō　感動

Literally: Everyone was *moved*.

• Mori-agatta　盛り上がった

This verb is frequently used of parties meaning something like *to take off, to heat up, to get going*.

• Consensus　コンセンサス

Ironic, perhaps, that this concept—the Japanese, after all, are respected internationally for achieving consensus before new projects go ahead, avoiding damaging conflicts between different sections of the same firm, and for troublefree management-labor relations—should be expressed with a foreign word.

• Neck　ネック

An abbreviation of bottle*neck*, this means an *obstacle*, a *point of difficulty*.

物知り英語ノート

• I'm shattered

本来は "粉々に砕かれた" という意味をもちますが、ここでは "非常に疲れた" ということを表現しています。他の言い方には次のようなものがあります。**I'm destroyed**（俺は破壊された）／**I'm whacked**（俺は打撃を受けた）／**I'm dead**（俺は死んだ）

• Were up all night／To be up all night

"徹夜する"

• Thank goodness

Thank God からきている言葉ですが、キリスト教でお祈り以外の時に神様の名前を借りるのは冒涜とみなされてしまいます。そこで **God** を **Goodness** に変えています。また、よく使われる **Gee** は **Jesus** からきています。

• Gung-ho

ガンホー、"熱烈、熱心" 第二次世界大戦中の米国の海兵隊の特徴を表わす形容詞で、元気、戦闘的なことを意味しています。**All out**（全力を傾けて）も同様に使うことができます。

• Superman

皆さんご存じのアメリカンコミックのヒーロー、スーパーマンです。チャックさんは渡部さんのプレゼンテーションの成功を賛え、渡部さんをなんでもできてしまう超人的な人と絶賛しています。

• Hairy

本来の意味は "毛深い" ですが、ここでは "しんどい、怖い" という表現に使われています。怖いことが起こると **Hair stands on end**（毛が逆立つ）ことからきています。

• Orgasmic

"興奮だらけ、興奮しまくり" ここでチャックさんは渡部さんのプレゼンが大成功だったと賛えるためにオーバーでちょっと下品な表現を使っています。

• Rock and roll

"盛り上がった"。この他に **Heat up**、**take off** も同じように使うこと
ができます。

• Fabulous

"素晴しい" ということを表現したい時、より長い単語を使うとそれを
発音するときにより感情のこもったものとなります。**Amazing／Brilliant／Superb／Excellent** も同じように使うことができますので、ぜ
ひ覚えて下さい。

• Achieving a consensus

"コンセンサスを得る" 日本の企業の場合、ミーティングで事を決定す
るよりも、ミーティング後の密談や根回しで決定することが多々ありま
す。従って日本では西洋に比べ意思決定に時間がかかります。

• Put a spanner in the works

"妨害する" 稼働している機械にスパナを差し込むと機械は止まってし
まいます。ここでは "富田さんが妨害する（スパナを入れる）だろう"
ということから、彼がネックになると渡部さんは確信しています。

8 | Marketing wa kuchi-saki dake na no ka?

Watanabe: Tomita-san, kono aida wa dōmo..., nani ka purezen [*presen*tation] ni kan shite...

Tomita: Omaera o yatotta toki, ore wa shachō ni iitan' da. Omaera ni **kitai shinai hō ga ii** 'tte. Konsarutanto [consultant] nan te **kuchi-saki** dake da, gyōkai ni tsuite nani mo chishiki ga nai kuse ni **erasō ni usankusai koto bakari o iu.** Anna **detarame** de hontō ni ore-tachi o **gomakasō** to omotte iru no ka? Are de kane o seikyū shiyō to omotte iru no ka!

Watanabe: Sumimasen. Are? kichatta zo!

Chuck: Dō shitan' desu ka? Yatto **ano jijii** no me kara mo uroko ga ochimashita ka?

Watanabe: **Mazutta!** **Yabai** koto ni natta ka mo!

Chuck: Nani ga atta no?

Watanabe: **Mukō** wa sugoku okotte iru rashii! Jigajisan de **mori-agatte,** purezen [*presen*tation] wa **bacchiri umaku itta** to omotteta no ni, jitsu wa, zenmen-shippai datta! **Mecha dame** da!!

Chuck: Chotto matte! Tomita kara monku no denwa ga atta koto wa betsu ni purezen [*presen*tation] ga shippai shita to iu koto o imi shite nain ja nai. Moshikashite, Tomita no tachiba ga tsuraku natte irun' de, katte ni denwa o ireta dake ja nai no. **Koitsu wa itazura denwa no sekai** da yo!

Watanabe: Maa, risutora [*restru*cture]de ichiban tachiba ga **shindoku** natte iru no wa, ano toroi yatsu da. Ano denwa wa kaisha-zentai no hannō de wa naku, hitori no zetsubō-teki-na jiko-bōei-kōi toshite mita hō ga ii ka...

Chuck: **Tondemonai hito desu ne!**

マーケティングは口先だけなのか

A sudden telephone call interrupts Chuck and Watanabe's cheerful (indeed we might even say self-congratulatory) review of their presentation. The mystery caller is none other than the evil Tomita, who informs them that the reactions to their strategy and naming presentations at Suzuki Denki were far less positive than they had imagined.

ワタナベ： 富田さん、この間はどうも…、なにかプレゼンに関して…

トミタ： おまえらを雇った時、おれは社長に言ったんだ。おまえらに期待しないほうがいいって。コンサルタントなんて口先だけだ、業界についてなにも知識がないくせに偉そうにうさん臭いことばかりを言う。あんなデタラメで本当に俺たちをごまかそうと思っているのか？あれで金を請求しようと思っているのか！

ワタナベ： すみません。　あれっ？　切っちゃったぞ。

チャック： どうしたんですか。やっとあのジジイの目からもウロコが落ちましたか？

ワタナベ： まずった！やばいことになったかも。

チャック： なにがあったの？

ワタナベ： 向こうはすごく怒っているらしい！自画自賛で盛り上がって、プレゼンはばっちりうまく行ったと思ってたのに、実は、全面失敗だった。めちゃダメだ！！

チャック： ちょっと待って！富田から文句の電話があったことは別にプレゼンが失敗したということを意味してないんじゃない。もしかして、富田の立場が辛くなっているんで、勝手に電話を入れただけじゃないの。こいつはいたずら電話の世界だよ。

The Superficiality of Marketing

興奮さめやらぬチャックさんと渡部さんのもとに1本の電話が入ります。なんと、あの富田副社長からです。富田副社長イコール鈴木電気ではないと理解しているふたりですが、プレゼンテーションの反応は思っていたよりよくなかったようです。

Watanabe: Mr. Tomita, good to hear from you... Is it something to do with the presentation?

Tomita: I told the boss when he hired you guys! I told him he **shouldn't expect much** from you! You consultants are just **big mouths**! You **get on your high horse**, and talk a lot of **nonsense** although you know nothing about the business itself! Do you really think **you can palm that pack of lies off** on us? Do you think you can bill us for that!

Watanabe: I'm very sorry... Eh? He's hung up on me.

Chuck: Hey what's up? Have the scales finally fallen from **the old fellow's** eyes?

Watanabe: Oh no! This is **really bad**!

Chuck: Did I miss something?

Watanabe: It looks as though the client is absolutely furious. I thought the presentation **had gone absolutely perfectly, there we were praising each other** and in fact it was a disaster! **What a mess**!

Chuck: Hey, hang on! The fact that Tomita called up to complain doesn't necessarily mean that your presentation was a failure. It's possible that since Tomita feels his position is under threat he called up on his own initiative. I tell you **it's like a prank call**!

ワタナベ： まあ、リストラで一番立場がしんどくなっている
のは、**あのとろいやつ**だ。あの電話は会社全体の反
応ではなく、一人の絶望的な自己防衛行為として
見たほうがいいか…

チャック： とんでもない人ですね！

Watanabe: Well, in the restructuring the guy who's position is going to be most **shaky** is **that moron**. Yeah, I should regard that call not as the reaction of the firm as a whole, but as one individual's desperate act of self-defence.

Chuck: **What a creep that guy is!**

Know-it-all Notes

• Kono aida wa dōmo　この間はどうも

Literally, "Thanks for last time," this greeting has no equivalent in English.

• Kuchi-saki　口先

All words and no action, just big talkers. Here Tomita is voicing the traditional Japanese distrust of freelancers as opposed to lifers, of thinkers as opposed to makers and doers.

• Kuse ni　くせに

No ni or ni mo kakarawazu also mean *although.* Not quite as offensive, however, as the tone implied by this one.

• Gomakasu　ごまかす

To cheat or *to bluff.* This verb originally meant to add sesame to food and so hide poor quality ingredients or lack of cookery skils. A bluffer or fraud is hattariya.

• Jijii　じじい

A colloquialization of *ojisan* or *oyaji.*

• Mazutta　まずった

A highly colloquial form of mazukatta. *Something awful's happened.*

• Kamo　かも

Understand as kamoshiremasen. *It maybe that...*

• Tondemonai hito　とんでもない人

An incredible guy! (in a negative sense) This is a handy self-deprecating expression. When complimented on the fluency of your Japanese, shake your head ruefully and mutter these words "Alas, far from it, far from it." Remember talking small works better than talking big in Japan.

• Good to hear from you

英語では日本語の「この間はどうも」「いつもお世話になっております」のような表現がありませんが、それらに一番近いものとしてこの **Good to hear from you** が挙げられます。ただし、この表現はある程度おつきあいのある方に対して使って下さい。

• You guys

友達同士で使うもので、日本語の"おまえら、あんたたち"に相当します。ビジネスの席で使う時は、相手に大変失礼な態度をとることになると覚悟して下さい。

• Big mouth

口が大きくてしゃべりまくるだけで内容のないことを意味します。**Big** はいろいろな慣用表現に使われています。**Big head**（うぬぼれや）**Big Wig**（大物）**Big Cheese**（大物社長やリーダー）

• Get on your high horse

直訳は大きな馬に乗るという意味。ここでは、"偉そうな態度をとる、うぬぼれる"。

• To palm off

"ごまかしを押し付ける"

• To bill

"請求する"

• He's hung up on me

"電話を切られた"。意識的に電話を切られた時に使います。何らかの理由で切れてしまった時は **The phone was cut off** を使います。

• Furious

"怒り狂った"。レベルの怒りの表現：**Irritated**（イライラする）→ **Angry**（怒る）→**Furious**（怒り狂う）／**Hopping mad**（飛び跳ねて怒る）

• Gone absolutely perfectly

"うまく行った"。日本語と同じように「行った」を **Go** で表わすことができます。**Be** 動詞を使いたければ **been a 100% success** といえます。

• A disaster

本来は災害という意味ですが、ここでは "大失敗" の意味です。これよりもっと大きな失敗は **A catastrophe** や **A fiasco** と言えます。**Didn't go well** では淡々として聞こえてしまい、それほど大失敗には聞こえません。

• What a mess!

Mess は部屋が乱雑、汚いときなどに使いますが、ここでは "まずいことになった" という意味で使われています。

• Hang on!

"ちょっと待って"。同じように **Slow down!／Wait a minute!** を使うことができます。

• The fact that...

"…ことは、必ずしも"

例：**The fact that he graduated from Todai doesn't necessarily mean he's intelligent**
「彼が東大を卒業したということは、必ずしも彼が頭のいい人だということを意味しない」（Chapter 3 参照）

• A prank call

いたずら電話。よく女性にかかるセックスを話題にしたいたずら電話は **Dirty Phone Call** といいます。

• Position is shaky

"立場が揺らいでいる、立場が危ない" の意味。

• Moron

Fool より一般的に使われている "ばかもの" という単語。

• Creep

本来の意味は虫などが "はう" ですが、虫が這っているのをみると気持ちが悪いのと同じように、ここでは富田さんを見ると "むしずが走る" という意味で使われています。

SEVEN

•

JUST SAY NO

NOと言えない日本

Ishihara Shintaro's book *The Japan That Can Say No* caused something of a sensation when published at the height of Japan's economic success in 1989. Ishihara and his coauthor Akio Morita of Sony assailed the United States as a degenerate floundering power, no longer worthy of imitation or obedience. Japan had outgrown its dependence on its now senile foster-parent, went the argument, and would henceforth follow it's own homegrown and superior way.

As was rather humiliatingly proven the subsequent year, Japan had in fact progressed only as far as being able to hum and haw and say "maybe," before concluding with its traditional meek "yes." When asked to contribute to the Gulf War, the government, torn between its self-image as a dove among war-hawks, and its very real dependence on oil imported from the Middle East contrived only to sit on the fence long enough to annoy all parties before forking over $10 billion.

The title of the book was thus a clever piece of marketing, but with little relation to reality. Whether at national or corporate level, the Japanese are simply not good at saying "No."

In a business context, the Japanese recognize when people who want to do business with them have worked hard, and are loath to disappoint them with a cold, straight "no." Consequently the negative, like an ageing Hollywood beauty queen, is filtered through a soft-focus lens, and the hard lines of dame, muri, and dekinai are blurred into the less jarring tones of tabun, chotto, kamoshirenai. But do not yield to optimism if someone tosses you the sop of a *maybe*, a *possibly*, or even a *probably*. That way madness lies! When Japanese businessmen have made up their minds to do something they speak briefly and clearly. So take this as your Golden Rule—

ANY ANSWER, HOWEVER POLITE, OTHER THAN "YES" AND A CONTRACT MEANS NO.

NO PLAY

It is important to recognize just how discreet the "no" can be. In its most wraith-like forms it appears at the tail end of a very positive remark as the apparently insignificant **ga,** followed by a slightly pained silence. For example—Onsha ga teiji shita project wa totemo omoshirokattan' desu **ga** (*We think your company's proposal to be most interesting BUT...*) **Do not delude yourself that the keyword is** *interesting.*

An equally discreet harbinger of bad news is chotto, *a little.* Should someone say to you "Sore wa chotto muri to omoimasu" (I think that's just *a little* impossible) **The** *a little* **is only intended to soften the disappointment you feel, and has no relation to degrees of impossibility.**

Another lurking-place of the "no" is in the verb of thinking or feeling employed. When things are straightforward people *think* (omou). When they are not happy they ki ga shimasu (have a feeling that), or yō na ki ga itashimasu (have a polite feeling that maybe), or kamoshirenai (think that may be). **Any excessively convoluted speech patterns, double negatives** (*the possible difficulties are not few*), **indirect questions** (*We ask our-*

selves can we really do this) **are best interpreted as a delicate "no," not as a request for a modification of the proposal itself.**

For the benefit of hypersensitive readers who cannot bear to disappoint even with the most indirect "no," we also include a selection of stale yet delicate pretexts for deferring the final decision. *In a large company reaching a decision always takes a long time* etc.

DELICATE NOs→EXCUSES→ DEFERRAL→NEXT TIME
デリケートなNO、口実、言い訳、延期

● ソンさんの提案はほんとに素晴しいと思いますが…

Son-san no teian wa honto ni subarashii to omoimasu **ga**…

We think your suggestions absolutely ingenious,
Mr. Son, **however**…

● 興味がないとは言えないですが…

Kyōmi ga nai to wa ienai desu ga…

While we are **not completely uninterested**…

● それはちょっと難しいような気がします…

Sore wa chotto **muzukashii yō na ki ga shimasu**…

We **feel** that **could be difficult**…

● どうもうまくいかないと思いますけど…

Dōmo umaku ikanai to omoimasu kedo…

I **just can't believe** it will work out well…

● 私の直感だけだけど、絶対にダメになると思うよ。

Watashi no **chokkan dake da kedo**, zettaini dame ni naru to omou yo.

This is no more than my gut-feeling, but I think it's bound to fail.

● 営業サイドが前例主義ですから…

Eigyō saido [side] ga **zenrei-shugi** desu kara…

The salesmen like to have **precedents**…

● それはうちの伝統にはまらない、わが社の精神に合っていない。

Sore wa uchi no **dentō ni hamaranai**, wagasha no seishin ni atte inai.

That just **doesn't fit in with our culture**, it just **doesn't match our philosophy**.

● もの自体がいくら素晴しくても、ちょっとタイミング的に早すぎるような気がいたします。

Mono jitai ga ikura subarashikute mo, chotto **taimingu [timing]-teki-ni hayasugiru** yō na ki ga itashimasu.

However good the product itself is, **I still have a sense that it's premature**.

- 今の段階ではちょっと決められないです。

Ima no dankai de wa **chotto kimerarenai desu.**

At the stage we're at just now I **don't think we can reach a decision**.

- 私には権限がないので、ちょっと上司と相談してからということでいかがでしょうか？

Watashi ni wa **kengen ga nai node,** chotto **jōshi to sōdan shite kara** to iu koto de ikaga deshō ka?

I'm sorry, but **since I'm not the decision-maker,** would it be OK if I came back to you **after consulting with my superiors**?

- そのへんについてはちょっと検討してからというかたちでよろしいでしょうか？

Sono hen ni tsuite wa chotto **kentō shite kara** to iu katachi de yoroshii deshō ka?

Would it be alright with you if we gave an answer **after considering that aspect** of the proposal somewhat more deeply?

- ちょっと今日話し合ったところを頭の中で整理して、違う面から考えてみましょう。

Chotto kyō hanashiatta tokoro o atama no naka de **seiri shite,** chigau men kara **kangaete mimashō.**

So let's reflect on what we talked about today and **try and put it in order**, then try and **look at this problem from a whole new angle**.

9 Tairyō-kaiko semaru

Watanabe: Ima made teian shita kakushinan wa shain no mae de disukasshon [discussion]-teki-na katachi de hanashimashita keredo...

Chuck: Kore kara torikumu-beki mondai wa, yori fukuzatsu de shain no mae de wa tori-agerarenai teema [theme] desu. Jinin-sakugen to iu koto desu kara.

Watanabe: Mazu, shōhin to senden o ikura yoku shite mo, kaisha no koteihi o herasanai to...

Chuck: Sore ni, chūnen no sutaffu [staff] yori, wakakute, yori yoku dejitaru [digital] gijutsu o rikai suru jinzai o yatowanai to.

Suzuki: Senryaku to shite totemo settokuryoku ni tonda, gori-teki-na mono desu **ga...**

Chuck: Sono "ga" wa, mijikai wari ni fukai imi demo aru no deshō ka?

Suzuki: Ima no Nihon de wa jinin-seiri wa **chotto muri da to omoimasu.** Kaisha wa kazoku mitai-na mono desu kara.

Chuck: Koteihi o herasanai to, kaisha-saisei ni hitsuyō-na setsubi-tōshi wa dekinain' desu.

Suzuki: Chōkiteki-ni kangaetara, hito o kubi ni suru koto de **samazama-na mondai ga hassei suru no de wa nai ka?**

Watanabe: Dono yō na mondai desu ka?

Suzuki: Maa, bōdaina taishokukin, rōdō-kumiai to no shōtotsu, soshite kaisha no mentsu no koto mo aru. Sore ni sengo no Nihon ni tairyō-kaiko no **zenrei ga nai** shi...

Chuck: Watashi no keisan ni yoru to, gojū-nin o katto [cut] shitara, koteihi o jū paasento [percent] herasu koto ga dekimasu. Kono ken ni kan shite, shachō-san wa do omowaremasu deshō ka?

Suzuki: Sore wa, **watashi ga ikura shachō demo**, **kono ba de wa kimerarenai. Sukoshi jikan o itadaka-nakereba**...

Watanabe: Koyō ni te o dasu koto ni taishite, shachō wa teikōkan o kanjite irassharu yō desu ne?

Suzuki: Sore wa sō desu yo!

Watanabe: Wakarimashita. Sore de wa koteihi o genshō saseru hōhō o o-tagai-ni **jikai made ni saikentō shimashō**.

大量解雇迫る

Till now Watanabe and Chuck have been making positive suggestions about how to improve the performance of Suzuki Denki. Here, however, in private conference with Suzuki, they are getting to grips with the delicate topic of cost-cutting. Will it be necessary for them to *let some people go?* Will we suddenly find ourselves without enough characters for subsequent chapters? Read on…

ワタナベ： 今まで提案した革新案は社員の前でディスカッションョン的な形で話しましたけれど…

チャック： これから取り組むべき問題は、より複雑で社員の前では取り上げられないテーマです。人員削減ということですから。

ワタナベ： まず、商品と宣伝をいくらよくしても、会社の固定費を減らさないと…

チャック： それに、中年のスタッフより、若くて、よりよくデジタル技術を理解する人材を雇わないと…

スズキ： 戦略としてとても説得力にとんだ、合理的なものですが…

チャック： その「が」は、短いわりに深い意味でもあるのでしょうか？

スズキ： 今の日本では人員整理はちょっと無理だと思います。会社は家族みたいなものですから。

チャック： 固定費を減らさないと、会社再生に必要な設備投資はできないんです。

A Delicate Debate on Downsizing

鈴木電気もリストラの中で一番難しいコスト削減、人員削減という
問題にとりかからなければなりません。アメリカ的、強気の経営を
プッシュするチャックさんに対し、鈴木社長ははっきりした態度を
とることができません。しかし、渡部さんは同じ日本人として鈴木
社長の気持ちが理解できるようです。

Watanabe: Up till now we've put forward all our ideas for changing the firm in front of the employees in a discussion style…

Chuck: The problem we have to deal with now is more delicate and so cannot be discussed in front of the staff. I'm talking about personnel cuts.

Watanabe: Basically, however good you make your product and your advertising, you have got to cut costs.

Chuck: In addition to that, instead of all these middle-aged people, you really should employ younger people, more familiar with digital technology.

Suzuki: Well, considered as pure strategy, it's highly persuasive and rational **BUT**…

Chuck: *Could it be that that "but" is highly meaningful, despite its brevity?*

Suzuki: In Japan nowadays letting people go **is simply still not possible**. You see a company is like a family…

Chuck: If you don't cut costs you won't be able to make the investments in plant essential for the company's revival.

スズキ： 長期的に考えたら、人をクビにすることでさまざまな問題が発生するのではないか？

ワタナベ： どのような問題ですか？

スズキ： まあ、膨大な退職金、労働組合との衝突、そして会社のメンツのこともある。それに戦後の日本に大量解雇の前例がないし…

チャック： 私の計算によると、50人カットしたら、固定費を10%減らすことができます。その件に関して、社長さんはどう思われますでしょうか？

スズキ： それは、私がいくら社長でも、この場では決められない。少し時間をいただかなければ…

ワタナベ： 雇用に手を出すことに対して、社長は抵抗感を感じていらっしゃるようですね。

スズキ： それはそうですよ！

ワタナベ： 分かりました。それでは固定費を減少させる方法をお互いに次回までに再検討しましょう。

Suzuki: But surely you'll acknowledge that looked at from a long-term perspective firing people **can lead to all sorts of problems**?

Watanabe: What kind of problems are those?

Suzuki: Well, huge retirement bonuses, clashes with the union, then there's the issue of the company's reputation. In post-war Japan **there's no precedent** for large-scale lay-offs.

Chuck: According to my calculations, if we cut fifty people, we can reduce costs by ten percent. What's your opinion on that, Mr. Suzuki?

Suzuki: For all my being the president, **that's not something I can decide here and now. I need time**…

Watanabe: It seems as though you are rather reluctant to tackle the thorny issue of employment. Would that be correct?

Suzuki: Yes, it most certainly would.

Watanabe: Right then. For the next time we meet **both sides should think of alternative ways** of cutting costs.

Know-it-all Notes

• Jinin-sakugen　人員削減

Reducing staff. Chuck could equally have used jinin-seiri, "cleaning up" or "tidying up the staff." Of course, while consultants and managers tend to use long and delicate euphemisms for "fire" and 'sack" in an effort to soften their remorse, those who are actually fired would use shorter, rougher terms like kubi, or katto [cut].

• Keihi o herasanai to　経費を減らさないと

Notice how the sentence just fades away with a to. *"However good your products and advertising, if you don't reduce costs… fade out to threatening silence.*

In the "Ode on a Grecian Urn" Keats reflected that "Things said are sweet, but those unsaid are sweeter." **In Japanese, things unsaid often have more impact**. If Chuck completed the second half of the sentence he would have to say *"If you don't… you will go bankrupt."* This would be rude and jarring, and *to say things as they really are* should be left for the last, desperate appeal (see Chapter 8).

• Gōriteki　合理的

Rational. It is difficult to know if Suzuki regards this as a dirty word or not. It's possible that he believes that there are more important things than cold reason necessary for managing a company successfully, to wit Ningen'mi (lit: *human flavor*, or *humanity*) and giri to ninjō (*duty* and *human-feeling*).

Remember, if Honda had been a rational accountant and not an enthusiast he would never have started on car-production in a mature market against the wishes of MITI. If Morita had listened to his colleagues he would never have produced the Walkman (see Chapter 10). One is reminded of Tom Peter's dictum, "To be narrowly rational is often to be negative… creative thought requires an act of faith."

• ga　が

Chuck comments aside that this word for all its being short is immensely significant. This is true of all particles in Japanese. It may help our readers to understand how the Japanese talk by looking at the poetry that Humpty Dumpty recites to Alice in *Through The Looking Glass.*

> But he was very stiff and proud:
> He said "You needn't shout so loud!"
> And he was very proud and stiff:
> He said "I'd go and wake them, **if—**"
> I took a corkscrew from the shelf:
> I went to wake them up myself:
> And when I found the door was locked,
> I pulled and pushed and kicked and knocked.
> And when I found the door was shut,
> I tried to turn the handle **but—**"
> There was a long pause.
> "Is that all?" Alice timidly asked.
> "That's all." said Humpty Dumpty. "Goodbye."
> This was rather sudden, Alice thought...

Notice the abruptness of the lines ending in "if" (**to**) and "but" (**ga**). Notice how Alice, since she comes from the other side of the looking glass, fails to get the message and has to ask "Is that all?" What an obtuse gaijin!

• Chotto muri　ちょっと無理

Japan may not be able to say no, but it is quite capable of saying "**chotto.**" Essentially it means "*apologetic* no." There are some charming uses, for example, a shopkeeper who has run out of something will say: **Ima wa chotto nai desu ne** (No I *a little bit* don't have any.) Degrees of nothing, ideed! The **chotto** should be accompanied by a tilting of the head and a grimace to emphasize the impossibility of the task, as well as to express the spiritual pain you feel in not being able to respond affirmatively.

• Rōdō-kumiai to no shōtotsu　労働組合との衝突

Smooth labor relations resulting from single company enterprise unions are generally considered one of the main reasons for Japan's postwar economic success. It remains to be seen if, in the age of white-collar job insecurity and less than headlong economic growth, the unions representing the office workers will be as easy to tame as the manufacturing unions were.

• Mentsu　メンツ

Face. Note the expressions Mentsu ga tatsu (gain face) and Mentsu ga tsubureru (to lose face). Although "face" is concept that writers on Japan get very excited about it is not spoken about that much, simply because everyone understands just how important it is. It literally *goes without saying*.

• Sengo no Nihon　戦後の日本

Suzuki is quite rightly making a distinction between before and after the war. Prewar Japan was distinguished by a huge gap between rich and poor, dependance upon cyclical industries and agriculture, and business was controlled by a few colossal family companies (zaibatsu). The smoothly cooperating society that we, and many Japanese, think of as "typical" is a freak child of postwar prosperity.

• Tairyō-kaiko　大量解雇

Large-scale lay-offs. Just as English has bland words such as "to let go," "to make redundant" that are generally used by the firer, but angry direct words like "be sacked," "be fired" that are used by the fired, so in Japanese a manager might use a delicate expression like kaiko (lit: the loosening of employment) while the sacked person would say he had had his *neck cut* (kubi ni sareta/kubi o kirareta).

• Kono ba de wa kimerarenai　この場では決められない

"I can't decide here, on the spur of the moment." Of course Suzuki really means no, he will never fire anyone. This is well understood by Watanabe who reads Suzuki's noncommittal remarks for the *no* they are.

物知り英語ノート

• However

"けど、が" という接続詞ではなく "いくら" という意味です。例え
ば：However clever you are you cannot avoid paying taxes forever いくら頭が良くても、いつまでも税金の支払を避け続けられない。

• Personnel cuts

人員削減を意味する言葉はたくさんあります。婉曲法を使った A
shake out、人間味に欠ける Downsizing、科学的な印象を与える
Reducing staff-levels、そのほかに Rationalizing the workforce、
Letting people go、美化したような表現として Making the firm
leaner and meaner などがあります。首を切られた人の立場からの表
現になると Fired、Sacked と意味のはっきりとした言葉が使われます。

• Cut costs

アメリカの企業では High profitability（高採算、高利益）を追及し、
good returns for investors "株主への高配当" を重視する傾向にあり
ます。このように株主への配当を心配するあまり、利益を重視し、研究
費などの経費を削減し、それらを株主に振り分けることを Quateritis
といいます。

• A company is like a family

多くの人々が終身雇用制は日本独特のものであると信じていますが、この
ようなシステムを初めて作ったのは IBM 社でした。(Chapter 10 参照)

• Like a family

アメリカでは dysfunctional family つまり、機能していないダメな家
族が多いので、リストラで苦労しているアメリカの会社も家族に似たも
のだと言えます。米国での離婚率は日本の3倍です。

• Large-scale lay-offs

"大量解雇" 円高が急激に進んだ90年代に、日本の名門企業はコスト削
減のために雇用に手を付けなければならないと騒がれましたが、アメリ
カ的なリストラを避けてきました。なぜなら日本では契約社員、女性社

員を解雇対象としたり、新入社員をとらないという対策を主とし、アメリカ的な大量解雇を回避することができたからです。

• Retirement bonuses

欧米で効率アップを目指し、会社をスリム化する時に **Restructuring costs**（リストラ費）が発生します。それはほとんどが解雇された人達への賠償金や退職金に当てられます。首を切られた時にもらうお金は **severance pay**（切られ金）と言います。

• Precedent

戦後、大量解雇が全くなかったということは間違いです。確かに、日本経済が軌道に乗ってからはありませんが、戦争直後の大混乱の中で、日本の責任感が強い大企業を代表する**マツシタ**は大勢の社員をカットしました。

• I need time

"時間が必要"　鈴木社長はコストの問題に直面したくないために時間稼ぎをしています。

• Thorny issue

"難しい問題" **Thorny** は "とげのある" を意味します。人員削減は非常にデリケートな問題です。チャックさんは気付いてないようですが、渡部さんは **It seems**（感じている）／**rather**（少し）／**reluctant**（遠慮）**Would that be correct?**（あってますか？）と間接的で丁寧な言い方で、鈴木社長に気を使いながら問題からの逃げ道を提供しています。

EIGHT

•

PILE ON THE PRESSURE
THE ELEMENTS OF
ELOQUENCE

誰も抵抗できない英語能弁法

Consider the following paradox: The foreigner who is seen reading the *Nihon Keizai Shimbun* will be regarded as the possessor of an awesome intellect, while he will in fact require to know a great deal less vocabulary than the reader of the more pungent tabloid press, whose semantic capacities must encompass all subjects from fornication to sumo wrestling and baseball.

This is the great secret of business Japanese—it is limited, finite, and circumscribed. A stockprice stays still, goes up or down. It cannot be spotted sneaking out of a love hotel dressed in a tracksuit at 2 a.m. A new product sells well, badly, or adequately. It does not murder in a frenzy and then distribute pieces of the dismembered corpse all over the countryside.

The downside of this easy-to-master terminology, however, is the danger of it becoming boring and repetitive. Where there is relatively little variety of action, it is important to introduce variety of language. Stocks must not just go up, they must rise *dramatically*, plunge *catastrophically*, or be *in the doldrums*. Following the dictum of its founder Bagehot to "simplify, then exaggerate," the British magazine *The Economist* has carried this style of speech to perfection, perhaps even to caricature.

1. ADVERBS
キー副詞

The first section of this chapter introduces adverbs to redeem your verbs from blandness. Note that while in English we can *significantly* increase the impact of a sentence by coupling a short verb with a polysyllabic adverb, the salaryman's favorite adverbs are of just two or three syllables, with a piercing ni at the end. The abundance of K, O, and Z sounds (e.g. **k**anpeki ni, jun'chō ni, **z**ettai ni) makes them easy to spit out with the necessary emphasis. For those so utterly and hopelessly attached to the polysyllabic adverb that they insist their addiction accompany them across the language barrier, there are a number that can be enjoyed in Japanese (e.g. attō-teki-ni, tettei-teki-ni, konpon-teki-ni). For the lazy, or hyperpragmatic, reader we recommend a species of telescopic adverb that can be reinforced with snap-on extensions (e.g. jūbun-ni, jūnibun-ni, jūhachibun-ni/*well, full well, more than full well*).

SHORT ADVERBS

● まだマイクロソフトを追い越すほどじゃないけど、
会社は結構うまく行っているよ。

Mada Maikurosofuto [Microsoft] o oi-kosu hodo ja nai
kedo, kaisha wa **kekkō** umaku itte iru yo!

I don't think we're out-performing Microsoft, but things
are going **pretty** well!

- 最初は少し大変だったが、今この仕事は順調に
  動いています。

Saisho wa sukoshi taihen datta ga, ima kono shigoto wa
junchō ni ugoite imasu.

At the start this was a pretty tough job, but it's going **pretty
smoothly** now.

- 我々が提供するサービスは御社のニーズにちょうど
  いいのではないかと思いますけど。

Wareware ga teikyō suru saabisu [service] wa onsha
no niizu [needs] ni **chōdo** ii no de wa nai ka to
omoimasu kedo.

We believe that the service we offer fits **perfectly** the needs
of your firm.

- 飽和状態、過当競争が騒がれているなかで、その
  メーカーの利益は好調に伸びている。

Hōwa-jōtai, katō-kyōsō ga sawagarete iru naka de, sono
meekaa [maker] no rieki wa **kōchō ni** nobite iru.

Despite all the panic about market saturation and excessive
competition, that manufacturers profits are increasing
at a good rate.

- あの課長は無口でも、相当のやり手だよ。

Ano kachō wa mukuchi demo, **sōtō no** yarite da yo.

Although that manager's rather quiet, he's a **real** achiever.

● 多くの場合、技術の者は営業のことをまったく
　　わかっていない。

Ooku no baai, gijutsu no mono wa eigyō no koto o
mattaku wakatte inai.

It's not uncommon for technical people to be **absolutely**
ignorant about sales.

● 地価暴落のせいで、不動産業界は非常に厳しい
　　状況にある。

Chika-bōraku no sei de, fudōsan-gyōkai wa **hijō ni kibishii**
jōkyō ni aru.

Owing to the freefall of land prices, property developers are
having a **really hard** time.

● ヒット商品が先進国に出れば、かならず発展途上国で
　　模造品が作られる。

Hitto [hit] shōhin ga senshinkoku ni dereba, **kanarazu** hat-
ten-tojōkoku de mozōhin ga tsukurareru.

If there's a hit product in the developed countries, **you can
guarantee** a fake will be made in the developing countries!

● あの会社は、競争力を守るため、現地生産にかなりの
　　力を入れている。

Ano kaisha wa, kyōsōryoku o mamoru tame, genchi-
seisan ni **kanari no** chikara o irete iru.

In order to remain competitive that firm's putting **a great deal
of** effort into local production.

LONG ADVERBS

● 流通のルートを**本格的に**考え直さないと、業績を上げる
ことは無理であろう。

Ryūtsū no rūto [route] o **honkaku-teki-ni** kangae-naosanai
to, gyōseki o ageru koto wa muri de arō.

Unless we **totally** rethink our distribution channels, I think it'll
be impossible to improve our results.

● サッチャーの革新政策があったにもかかわらず、
英国の経済は**根本的に**ダメだと言って
いいのではないでしょうか？

Sacchaa [Thatcher] no kakushin-seisaku ga atta ni mo
kakawarazu, Eikoku no keizai wa **konpon-teki-ni**
dame da to itte ii no de wa nai deshō ka?

Despite Mrs. Thatcher's reforms, would it not be fair to say
that the British economy is **basically** finished?

● ソフト業界では今のところマイクロソフトが**圧倒的に**
強いといっても、それがどのぐらい
続くのかは、わかりません。

Sofuto [soft] gyōkai de wa ima no tokoro Maikurosofuto
[Microsoft] ga **attō-teki ni** tsuyoi to itte mo, sore ga
dono gurai tsuzuku no ka wa wakarimasen.

In the software business right now Microsoft is **overwhelm-
ingly** the strongest player. How long this state of affairs
will last is open to question.

SNAP-ON ADVERBS

● ビデオゲームの教育的なベネフィットは消費者に
十分伝わっていない。

Bideo-geemu [video game] no kyōiku-teki-na benefitto
[benefit] wa shōhisha ni **jūbun** tsutawatte inai.

The educational benefits of video games are not yet
sufficiently well understood by consumers.

● ライバル会社の一挙一動に注意する必要があることは、
十二分にわかっている。

Raibaru [rival] kaisha no ikkyo-ichidō ni chūi suru hitsuyō
ga aru koto wa **jūnibun ni** wakatte iru

We understand **full well** the importance of watching our
rivals' every move.

● 60年代、日本の会社はすごい勢いで成長した。

Rokujū-nendai, Nihon no kaisha wa **sugoi** ikioi de
seichō shita.

In the 1960s Japanese firms grew **with tremendous** vigor.

● ハードに比べて、ソフトの利益マージンはものすごく
高いですよ！

Haado [hard] ni kurabete, sofuto [soft] no rieki maajin
[margin] wa **monosugoku** takai desu yo.

Compared to hardware, the profit margins on software are
just unbelievably high.

2. ONOMATOPOEIA
キー擬声語／擬態語

Japanese onomatopoeic words (buyon-buyon, mero-mero, kya-kya, buu-buu) though numerous (we have well over 1000 in our dictionary!) are so full of childish zest that they seem an anomaly in such a formal society as Japan. Many Japanese onomatopoeic expressions did, in fact, originate in Polynesia and thus have a kind of lusty innocence more redolent of a beach paradise than the gloomy steppe of the open-plan office.

Why then, you ask, should the besuited businessman wish to use such childish and naive language in his presentations? Why commute to Otemachi, Tokyo's financial center, in a dugout canoe?

The answer is simple. Onomatopoeic expressions are highly expressive and emphatic (like the vulgar language of Chapter 6, onomatopoeic terms can achieve a rhetorically effective change of tone). They also sound sincere and unaffected. Certain onomatopoeic expressions (such as kichin-to, pishitto) have even become commonplaces in the business world.

● アフターサービスを**キチン**としないと、お客さんを
維持するのは難しい。

Afutaa-saabisu [after service] o **kichin to** shinai to,
o-kyaku-san o iji suru no wa muzukashii.

If you don't do your after sales service **just right**, it's difficult
to retain your customers.

● 韓国の会社はこわい存在ですよ！どんどん
　　追い付いてくるよ！

Kankoku no kaisha wa kowai sonzai desu yo! **Dondon**
oi-tsuite kuru yo!

Those Korean companies are terrifying! They're gaining on
us **all the time**!

● 創造性に乏しい、気が小さい団塊の世代はズルズル
　　仕事をすることしかできない。

Sōzōsei ni toboshii, ki ga chiisai dankai no sedai wa
zuruzuru shigoto o suru koto shika dekinai.

Those uncreative, spiritless men of the "group-think"
generation! All they can do is **beaver away
slavishly** at their work.

● 会社のなかで自己主張、つまり自分の意見を遠慮なく
　　言うことは徐々に浸透して来た。

Kaisha no naka de jikoshuchō, tsumari jibun no iken o
enryo naku iu koto wa **jojo** ni shintō shite kita.

Self-assertiveness, in short the habit of daring to say what you
think, has **gradually** filtered through the firm.

● 日本経済がすっかり再生するには、思いきった
　　規制緩和が必要だ。

Nihon-keizai ga **sukkari** saisei suru ni wa, omoikitta
kisei-kanwa ga hitsuyō da.

For Japan to recover **completely**, very bold deregulation
is necessary.

- 東京で騒がれたテリヤキバーガーが米国で発売
された時、あまりパッとしなかった。

Tōkyō de sawagareta teriyaki baagaa [burger] ga Beikoku de hatsubai sareta toki amari **pat-to** shinakatta.

The "Teriyaki burger" that had been such a success in Tokyo **hardly made a stir** when it was launched in the States.

- 今回のプレゼンをバッチリ決めて、この契約を
ピシっと取りましょう。

Konkai no purezen [*presen*tation] o **bacchiri** kimete, kono keiyaku o **pishit-to** torimashō.

Let's do this presentation **perfectly** and **sew up** this contract.

3. COMPOUND VERBS
複合動詞／ダブル・トラブル・動詞

If Japanese adverbs tend to be shorter than their English equivalents, this is compensated for by the ease with which the Japanese can create, and the frequency with which they use, compound verbs. Let us examine how a compound verb differs in tone from a simple verb.

Consider the verbs dekiru (to complete) and deki-agaru (to complete) in the sentence Watashi wa sono shigoto o deki-ta/deki-agatta (*I have completed that task*). If these two verbs were exact synonyms, then a syllable-conscious foreigner with a limited memory capacity would tend to plump for the shorter alternative, dekiru.

He or she would be **WRONG!** The effect of the added -agaru is to suggest that the work you completed was taihen (terribly hard) and required much dōryoku (blood, sweat, and tears), but has nonetheless been completed to a high degree of kanseido (perfection). If you have merely dekita'd the work, the suggestion is that you regarded the task as contemptibly easy and did not suffer in the doing of it. Compound verbs give an Homeric quality to your actions. You have captured a market as if it were Troy, you have vanquished a rival company as Achilles killed Hector, you have dallied with hostesses in bars as Paris did with Helen... It is important to suffer in Japan. If you finish your work promptly and easily, you will not serve as an inspiration, but as a depressant to your colleagues!

● 高齢化社会による人手不足への対策を打ち出さ
なければならない。

Kōreika-shakai ni yoru hitode-busoku e no taisaku o **uchi-dasanakereba naranai**.

We have **to come up with** a policy to address the problem of labor shortages caused by the ageing of society.

● アメリカの自動車産業に将来がないとは
言い切れないと思う。

Amerika no jidōsha-sangyō ni shōrai ga nai to wa **ii-kirenai** to omou.

I don't think you can **declare outright** that American car manufacturers are finished.

● 本物の企業家には、まだ出ていない市場のニーズを
　　見通せる能力がある。

Hon-mono no kigyōka ni wa, mada dete inai shijō no niizu
[needs] o **mi-tooseru** nōryoku ga aru.

A true entrepreneur has the ability to **see** the needs of
a market that doesn't yet exist.

● 狂牛病のせいで、牛肉の人気が急速に落ちたんです。
　　それをどう乗り切るかが今年の課題です。

Kyōgyūbyō no sei de, gyūniku no ninki ga kyūsoku ni
ochitan' desu. Sore o dō **nori-kiru** ka ga
kotoshi no kadai desu.

Owing to mad cow disease the popularity of beef has
plummeted. The big question we have to face
this year is how to **overcome** this.

4. METAPHORS OF WAR & BATTLE

戦争や戦士：サラリーマンのセルフ・イメージ・アップ効果隠喩

In his classic *The Affluent Society*, John Kenneth Galbraith pointed out how in the highly conservative, hierarchical, and risk-
averse giant corporations of the United States *of that time*, the
average salaried employee, who had nothing to look forward to
but a life of stable employment and rising remuneration, added
color to his self-image by the enthusiastic adoption of military
terminology. He wasn't a desk-bound non-entity in a gray suit
surrounded by thousands of clones. He was a Napoleon who
devised *strategies* and *campaigns* in the *headquarters*, who made
marketing *offensives*, and who *pushed into* new countries.

While the American corporation, agitated by boardroom coups and massive lay-offs, has come to resemble a third world army, with generals disappearing suddenly in the night and the rank and file periodically decimated to set an example for others, the giant and gigantically stable corporation, the bland organization man of William H. Whyte, and the military metaphor have all crossed over intact to Japan.

Conspiracy theorists like to regard Japan's trade success as war by other means. We are told that the Ministry of War discreetly metamorphosed into the Ministry of Trade and Industry, that Japan's economic hegemony in Asia is a recreation of the pre-war Pan-Asia Co-Prosperity Sphere. In newspaper cartoons, Japan is invariably represented as either the battling sumo wrestler or the sword-wielding samurai. John Connor, the detective-cum-Japanologist in Michael Crichton's *Rising Sun* declares "All's fair in love and war, and the Japanese see business as war."

The Only Pleasure is Pain

It is important to note the number of words in this section that include the kanji ku (suffering) for example akusenkuto/kusen/kurō. If the Japanese salaryman does indeed regard himself as a soldier he is no samurai, no officer, but some much put-upon infantry man up to his neck in a sludgey trench, for whom war is hell. (The war analogy with the all male company, the heavy drinking, and the leniency with which sexual excess is regarded, works rather well!) However the Japanese are not really averse to a little discomfort. Appropriately for a nation that isn't much good at having fun, they enjoy complaining. In this they are very similar to that other great island nation, the British. But whereas the British complain *instead of* working, the Japanese work and *then* relax by complaining. The latter approach tends to foster a more thriving economy.

This section will introduce you to ten or so of the commonest metaphors of war, battle, blood, sweat, and tears used in the Japanese business world.

● 営業戦士を定義するの？やっぱし、過労死するまで
　頑張ることが最も大きな特徴ではないか？

Eigyō-senshi o teigi suru no ? Yappashi, karōshi suru made
ganbaru koto wa mottomo ookina tokuchō de wa nai ka?

You want me to define "**the sales samurai?**" Well, I guess their
most important feature is to fight on and on till they die of
overwork, isn't it?

● VHSとベータの間の競争は文字どおりの**死闘**でした。

VHS to Beta no aida no kyōsō wa moji doori no
shitō deshita.

The competition between VHS and Betamax was literally
a fight to the death.

● 成績が落ちた時、そのコンピュータ会社はMBAの
　精鋭を営業に移した。

Seiseki ga ochita toki, sono konpyūta [computer] kaisha
wa MBA no **seiei** o eigyō ni utsushita.

When its performance went downhill that company shifted all
the MBA **crack soldiers** into sales.

● **完全無敵**だと思われていたドイツの工作機械業界は
　最近、日本メーカーの**攻撃**に**苦労**しています。

Kanzen-muteki da to omowarete ita Doitsu no kōsakukikai-
gyōkai wa saikin, Nihon meekaa [maker] no **kōgeki** ni
kurō shite imasu.

Recently the German machine tools sector, once **hailed as
invincible**, is **hurting badly** under the Japanese **assault**.

Suzuki-shachō no kandō-teki speech

Suzuki: Mina-san go-zonji da to omoimasu ga, sūnen-mae kara wagasha no keiei wa **taihen mondai o kakaete orimashite, kikikan o idaite inai** shain nado hotondo inakatta to iu no wa **tōzen** no koto de arimasu. Sono riyū wa, shijō no **kakiteki-na** henka, tsumari, shōhisha ga waa-puro [*word-pro*cessor] o hitsuyō to shinaku natta koto ni arimasu. Sore ga ima, wagasha no **shikatsu-mondai** ni natte imashite, sugu ni nani ka **te o uttanai** to **o-shimai** da, to iu koto ga akiraka ni narimashita. Mina-san ga Ameri-ka-teki-na risutora [*restru*ture] o osorete iru koto wa **jūbun** wakarimasu ga, wareware ga kangaete iru no wa seichō ni motozuita pojitibu [positive]-na risutora [*restru*ture] de arimasu.

Omoikitte, kaisha o **yari-naosanai** to rokujūnen no rekishi o hokoru Suzuki Denki ga nakunaru osore mo arimasu. Soko de shijō-henka ni teikō sezu, sore o chansu [chance] to shite miru **maemuki**-na, **tōshi** ni michita **eigyō-sen-shi** ni fusawashii kangaekata o mina-san ni motte hoshi! Kono atarashii gijutsu no kaihat-su ni **chikara o irete,** Watanabe-san ga teian shita maaketingu [marketing] senryaku o **buki ni shite,** mō ichido **tatakaimashō! Shōbu no michi wa kibishii** desu ga, Nihon no kigyō no rekishi wa kon'nan no **kabe o kiri-kuzusu** koto, **daitan ni shingijutsu ni tobi-tsuku** koto, **omoikitte atarashii bunya ni fumi-kiru** koto de tsukurarete kimashita. Watashi-tachi mo, korekara subarashii nijūi-seiki-gata no kaisha o **kizuki-agete ikitai** to omoimasu.

Chuck: Shachō wa **kanpeki ni** jukugo jankii [junkie] ni henbō shita no ka?

鈴木社長の感動的スピーチ

As a result of Chuck and Watanabe's eloquence (and no doubt the extraordinary power of Microsoft Windows) Suzuki has finally been convinced of the wisdom of McVitie Consulting's recommendations. He announces his decision to implement their brand strategy to the assembled staff. A company with a great history like Suzuki Denki must not be allowed to fade away!

スズキ： 皆さんご存じだと思いますが、数年前から我が社の経営は大変問題を抱えておりまして、危機感を抱いていない社員などほとんどいなかったというのは当然のことであります。その理由は、市場の画期的な変化、つまり、消費者がワープロを必要としなくなったことにありました。それが今、我が社の死活問題になっていまして、すぐに何か手を打たないとおしまいだ、ということが明らかになりました。皆さんがアメリカ的なリストラを恐れていることは、十分わかりますが、我々が考えているのは成長に基づいたポジティブなリストラであります。

思いきって、会社をやり直さないと60年の歴史を誇る鈴木電気がなくなる恐れもあります。そこで市場変化に抵抗せず、それをチャンスとしてみる前向きな、闘志に満ちた営業戦士にふさわしい考え方を皆さんにもってほしい！この新しい技術の開発に力を入れて、渡部さんが提案したマーケティング戦略を武器にして、もう一度戦いましょう！勝負の道は厳しいですが、日本の企業の歴史は困難の壁を切り崩すこと、大胆に新技術に飛びつくこと、思いきって新しい分野に踏み切ることで作られてきました。私たちも、これから素晴らしい21世紀型の会社を築き上げていきたいと思います！

チャック： 社長は完璧に熟語ジャンキーに変貌したのか？

Suzuki Rallies the Troops

チャックさんと渡部さんのコンサルティングを受け、ウインドウズのパワーを確信し、会社再生のために一大決心をした鈴木社長は、社員に対し会社の今後に関してのスピーチを行っています。自分のスピーチにのめり込み演説口調になっている鈴木社長は、社員を盛り上げようとレトリックを目指しています。

Suzuki: As you are all no doubt aware, for a number of years this company has been **grappling with tremendous problems**. As a result almost all of you have been **gripped by a sense of crisis**. The reason? **A sea-change** in the market—basically consumers have decided that they don't want word-processors anymore. This is now **a question of life and death** for us and it's quite clear that **if we don't take action now we're finished**! I understand **full well** that you are afraid of an American-style restructuring, however what we are planning is a positive kind of restructuring based on growth.

If we do not act **boldly** now to **reorganize** the firm, Suzuki Electronics, with its proud 60 year history, will just vanish. So, then, I want you not to resist changes in the market, but to consider changes to be opportunities. Cultivate **a forward-looking, do-or-die mindset**, a mindset worthy of a **sales samurai**! So, **let's put everything we have** into developing this new technology, and with the marketing strategy proposed by Watanabe **as a secret weapon**, **let's get out there and kick butt** again! It will be **a tough struggle**! But the history of Japanese industry is a story composed of **smashing through and tearing down** the walls of problems, of **boldly getting to grips** with new technology, of **courageously venturing into** new fields. Now together let us build a company fit for the 21st century!

Chuck: The boss has metamorphosed into something of a rabble-rousing demagogue!
(Lit: compound word junkie)

Know-it-all Notes

- **Go-zonji** ご存じ

The polite form of shiru, to know. Note the polite expression, go-zonji no yō ni, ("as you are all aware") which is a handy one to throw out from time to time at meetings.

- **Kikikan** 危機感

Feeling of crisis. The Japanese are fond of feeling a sense of crisis, whether due to hikes in the price of oil (1973), or dramatic leaps in the rise of the yen (1985 and 1994). Their feelings of crisis provide a spur to action, thus a kiki—composed of the kanji for danger and opportunity—may ultimately be a good thing, leading to cost-cutting measures that make Japanese industry even more fearfully efficient.

- **Shikatsu-mondai** 死活問題

A problem of life and death.

- **Oshimai** おしまい

"'The end" but rather theatrical—something like "it's curtains for us!"

- **Positive risutora** ポジティブなリストラ

A very quaintly Japanese interpretation of restructuring which, when all the dust of buzzwords has settled, invariably provides enormous leaps in productivity only at the cost of massive job losses. Suzuki is obviously expecting to become a market leader in PCs, and thus avoid the unpleasantness of sacking anyone.

While by no an means out-and-out fan of Peter Drucker with his relentless displays of learning and his overbold generalizations so typical of the auto-didact, I do agree wholeheartedly with his views on "downsizing."

"What is new and by no means desirable is the way in which these layoffs are being carried out. This is what bothers me. A lot of top managers enjoy cruelty. There's no doubt that we are in a period in which you are a hero if you are cruel. In addition, what's absolutely unforgivable is the financial benefit top management gets for laying off people. There's no excuse. No justification. No explanation. This is morally and socially unforgivable and we'll pay a very nasty price." (*Wired* August 1996)

• Omoikitte   思いきって

Boldly, wholeheartedly, in one go. We could equally have used omoikiri here.

• Yari-naosanai to   やり直さないと

"To start all over again," "to have a second start." Along with kangae-naosu one of the salaryman's all time favorite verbs.

• Shōbu no michi wa kibishii   勝負の道は厳しい

"Winning isn't easy," or "it's a long and hard road to success."

• 21-seiki-gata no kaisha   21世紀型の会社

What is a *twenty-first-century-style company*? Suzuki has no idea, but it will serve as a rallying cry for the troops (see Dialogue 5).

• Kizuki-agete ikitai   築き上げていきたい

This form of main verb + ikitai/iku is used to talk about what you intend to do in the future. To describe your achievements up till the present use main verb te-form + kita.

• Jukugo   熟語ジャンキー

Compound word. Whether anyone who overhears Chuck's indiscreet remark will understand the word *Junkie* is not clear. Unlike some other Asian countries where heroin and opium are produced and consumed in large quantities, Japan has few hard drug addicts. If one looked, however, at addiction to tobacco, alcohol, sickly sweet canned coffee, energy-drinks, and work the picture would be grimmer.

物知り英語ノート

- ## American-style restructuring

アメリカ式リストラは、利益率を向上させる効果をもたらすことで注目を浴びています。リストラの最初に行われる措置は、必ずといっていいほど大量解雇です。従って、アメリカ式リストラと聞くと社員が恐怖感を持つのも当然です。

- ## Do-or-die

19世紀のテニソン（イギリス）が書いた詩から。**Yours not to reason why, Yours just to do or die**（なぜと理由を聞くよりも戦うか、死ぬかだ！）

- ## Sales Samurai

欧米の新聞の1コマまんがを見ると、たいていアメリカ人はアンクルサム又はカウボーイ、日本人はサムライ又は力士に代表されています。外務省によると、80年代は日本の威力を象徴するような大型の力士、経済的に落ちこんでいる時はやせぎみの侍とのこと。

- ## The history of Japanese industry

ごく最近まで西洋人が持っていた戦後の日本急成長のイメージは、イミテーション（西洋をまねする）というものでしたが、**Fax** や **Walkman** の開発によりその開発技術の真価が認められるようになりました。また、トヨタ自動車が1950年頃から開発、実施している生産管理、在庫管理システムの一部であるカンバン方式は、テーラー・システム、フォード・システムに次いで誕生した独自の生産方式でした。カンバン方式イコール **Just in Time method** といわれていますが、正確にはカンバン方式は生産システムを構成するサブシステムです。マサチューセッツ工科大学のウーマック教授はトヨタの生産方式を **Lean production** システムとよんでいます。**Lean** はぜい肉がない、筋肉質という意味をもちます。

NINE

●

INSTANT WISDOM
(OF THE CONVENTIONAL KIND)

世間一般に受けいれられた考え方

---

*Why should **I** wish to spout cliches & commonplaces?*

Although Japan is a country where the pace of innovation never slows, and new products stream hurryingly direct from television commercials into obsolescence, the pace of intellectual change is stately, if not stumbling. While the British consumer might be content with a ten-year old television and a five-year old car, he will always be demanding *new* music, *new* fashions, *new* species of hypervitriolic comedy. Ideas, as well as products, get outmoded. Things that are excessively fashionable become, by virtue of their success, unfashionable. Things that everybody says come to ring untrue.

With the exception of the world of manufacturing, however, this principle of built-in obsolescence does not hold good in Japan. Perennial favorites are everywhere. The unfortunate *gaijin*, pressed into visiting a karaoke salon, can enjoy a wide selection of ...Frank Sinatra, Elvis, or the Beatles. He will be informed by many that *The Sound of Music* is their favorite film. Audrey Hepburn, despite being dead, still contrives to appear in television commercials. Equally, foreigners can soon learn to predict with what kind of small talk they shall be entertained. Of Germans, it will invariably be asked if they really do eat potatoes and drink beer all the time. The Englishman shall be crammed *willy-nilly* into the gentleman stereotype, as if soccer hooligans and skinheads had never existed. Meanwhile, the American, depending on his hair color, but quite regardless of his looks, will be found to resemble either Tom Cruise or Harrison Ford.

Such "oldies but goldies" exist also in the world of business philosophy, and the purpose of this chapter is to introduce you to a wide variety of remarks rich in conventional wisdom. In a Japanese company it is fair to say that staff under thirty are not usually permitted to be wise, even conventionally so, but, the more senior you are, the greater the solemnity with which you can produce unoriginal remarks. Since the purpose of Japanese meetings is seldom to discuss things, but to put them on the table, to air them or *absorb them by osmosis* what is actually verbalized probably does not matter that much. Thus, ultimately, silence, a grunt, or a commonplace are pretty much the same thing.

Commonplaces, however, do have several merits. Firstly, they provide covering fire giving you time to think. Secondly, they soothe and reassure your business counterparts that you are one of them, and not some terrifying T. Boone Pickens or Michael Milken Anti-Christ-of-the-business-world figure. Thirdly, provided your audience is not too shrewd, the adept insertion of some conventional wisdom can impart to you an air of immense sagacity, of off-the-cuff omniscience. In short, you can gain time, gain trust, and gain respect.

In order to assist you to share the insights of the business community we have analyzed and categorized the most popular gems of conventional wisdom. This exercise has yielded six categories, which are set out on the chart below for maximum intelligibility.

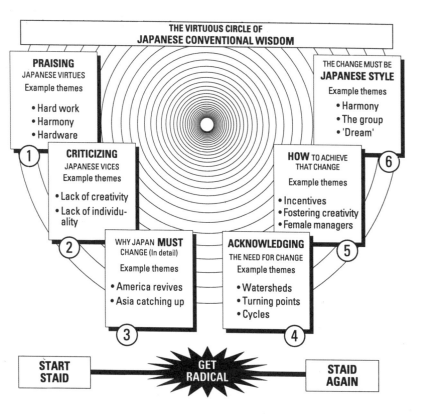

THE VIRTUOUS CIRCLE OF JAPANESE CONVENTIONAL WISDOM

PRAISING
JAPANESE VIRTUES
Example themes

• Hard work
• Harmony
• Hardware

1

CRITICIZING
JAPANESE VICES
Example themes

• Lack of creativity
• Lack of individuality

2

WHY JAPAN **MUST** CHANGE (In detail)
Example themes

• America revives
• Asia catching up

3

THE CHANGE MUST BE
JAPANESE STYLE
Example themes

• Harmony
• The group
• 'Dream'

HOW TO ACHIEVE THAT CHANGE
Example themes

• Incentives
• Fostering creativity
• Female managers

6

ACKNOWLEDGING
THE NEED FOR CHANGE
Example themes

• Watersheds
• Turning points
• Cycles

5

4

START STAID

GET RADICAL

STAID AGAIN

Notice: Some rather weedy foreigners will insist you are a guest in Japan and therefore have no business to do anything but praise the Japanese. This stance shows not only a lack of guts, but a lack of insight. The Japanese enjoy criticizing themselves and being criticized. Self-flagellation insures that they won't slacken in the global economic race, and ultimately, whatever they practice they adopt from abroad, they shall always fuse them with something Japanese anyhow, to make them unique, &c&c...

Let us now run through these categories one by one in greater detail.

1. PRAISING JAPANESE VIRTUES
日本・イズ・ナンバー・ワン

This category can be dealt with briefly and conveniently with a mnemonic. When praising Japan, one must praise the three H's—to wit, *harmony*, *hard work*, and *hardware*.

Does this clump of clichés really need any elaboration? Japanese businessmen achieve a kind of harmony by not (unless they are the president) taking decisions on their own. After due **nemawashi**-*ing* and **ringisho**-*ing*, responsibility will have been divided into so many little bits that ultimately no one person is liable for any divisive praise or blame. To reach a decision thus takes a very long time.

We all know that the Japanese work hard, or at least, as cynics would have it, are physically present in the office for many hours a day.

As regards hardware, the dominance of the Japanese needs no explanation, just listing a few brand names (Sony, Fujitsu, Toshiba, Panasonic) is enough. Recently articles (with titles like "The Japanese Key Devices Supporting America's Multimedia Boom") showing just how reliant American computer giants are on Japanese components have been appearing in the press.

● 日本の会社では調和を大切にする傾向が強いです。

Nihon no kaisha dewa chōwa o taisetsu ni suru keikō ga tsuyoi desu.

Japanese firms tend to regard **harmony** as very important.

● うちの会社の伝統は何だと聞かれると「和」と
　　答えるしかない。

Uchi no kaisha no dentō wa nan da to kikareru to **"Wa"** to
kotaeru shika nai.

If someone asks me what our company's tradition is, I've just
got to reply "preserving **harmony**."

● 今までの日本は**集団主義**だった。**協力**と**協調**が
　　キーワードだった。

Ima made no Nihon wa **shūdan-shugi** datta. **Kyōryoku** to
kyōchō ga kiiwaado [keyword] datta.

Until recently Japan was very **group-oriented**. The big things
were cooperation and helping each other out.

● 我々日本人は**働き者**だよ。我々より**一生懸命**働く
　　人間はこの世にいないぞ。

Wareware Nihonjin wa **hatarakimono** da yo. Wareware
yori **isshōkenmei** hataraku ningen wa kono yo ni inai zo!

Japanese people are **hard workers**. There's no one works harder than us on the planet!

● 日本はやっぱりハードの面がすごいよ!

Nihon wa yappari **haado [hard]** no men ga sugoi yo!

Japan produces incredible **hardware**!

2. CRITICIZING JAPANESE VICES
日本の欠点を攻める

This negative category is considerably larger than its positive predecessor suggesting that the Japanese in addition to having a masochistic streak, recognize the value of avoiding complacency by healthy doses of self-criticism. The most sweeping criticism in which one is permitted to indulge is a general lament about the degeneracy of the young. It is felt (and appears to have been felt for several decades of consistent economic growth) that the young Japanese lack the sturdy work ethic of their fathers.

While it is true that the majority of companies no longer work a six-day week (as they do, say, in Korea) the great distinction between Japan and other developed western economies, is that enthusiasm and a sense of responsibility for the job are felt at all levels of the organization. Thus, with the exception of office ladies at larger companies who serve a larger, *eugenial* role, no one will go home on time. It is not merely the overpaid who do overtime.

I am inclined to think that the myth of a decline in moral fibre is due only to an increase in the conspicuousness of leisure. Whereas the salaryman of the 1950s might take a trip to a hot-spring, or drink himself unconsciousness in Shinjuku, both would leave only temporary traces—the former resulting in a healthy flush, the latter in a ghastly pastiness of the complexion. Now, by contrast, a holiday taken abroad may produce some unignorable result, like a suntan: A hobby may involve some large and hard-to-conceal piece of equipment like a surfboard, or a pair of skis. Such material evidence of the conspicuous consumption of leisure (for all that conspicuous production continues unabated) give off a faint whiff of degeneracy, of **butsuyoku** (lust for things, materialism). The older members of society strove to rebuild their country from the ashes, to feed their families, to send their children to university, and are, I think, unhappy to see the pursuit of those noble, austere, and somewhat abstract goals, culminate, to borrow Baudrillard's phrase, in no more than an orgy of perpetual shopping.

Slightly graver than these concerns over an illusory degeneracy, is the feeling that the young have become strange, soulless beings. Occasionally an older Japanese will be found, like Dr. Frankenstein, shaking his head and asking himself *what monster he has created*. The argument goes that young Japanese are obliged to study so much and to leap through so many hoops that their humanity has been damaged or extinguished. They pass exams not for love of learning, but… because *the exams are there*. They join a certain company, not because they love what it makes, but because *that is what one must do*. This passivity is felt to contrast unfavorably with the rugged self-will of men like Soichiro Honda and Akio Morita, who often built their companies in the face of opposition from the bureaucracy.

The old, however, do not spare themselves the rod of criticism. Is the relative decline of Japanese growth rates perhaps due to their fear of risk? Are middle-aged *buchos* all across the land stifling the natural creativity of youth by insisting on adhering to models that served them well up till now, but are not guaranteed to serve them well in the future? How can a section chief lead his subordinates' charge into the information society if he, suffering from "keyboard allergy" has never touched a computer in his life?

Happy Flagellation!

● 日本の場合、何でもパターン化／定型化されています。

Nihon no baai, nandemo **pataan [pattern]-ka/teikei-ka** sarete imasu.

In the case of Japan, somehow or other everything becomes **formalized/rigidly structured**.

● 日本で個性の発揮は難しいと言える。

Nihon de **kosei no hakki** wa muzukashii to ieru.

In Japan you could argue it's difficult to be an **individual**.

● 日本だったら「周りが反対するだろうからやめておこう」ということになる。

Nihon dattara "**mawari ga hantai suru** darō kara yamete okō" to iu koto ni naru.

People tend to **fear what those around them will think**, so abandon putting forward their own ideas.

● 日本の経済を締め殺しているのは、創造性の全くないオヤジ族だ。

Nihon no keizai o shime-koroshite iru no wa, sōzōsei no nai **oyaji-zoku** da.

The people really suffocating in the Japanese economy are all those **dreary middle-aged managers**.

● あいつがクビにならずに部長になったのは、
　年功序列と終身雇用のせいだ。

Aitsu ga kubi ni narazu ni buchō ni nattano wa, **nenkō-joretsu** to **shūshin-koyō** no sei da.

The only possible reason that guy became a department chief rather than get fired is because of the Japanese system of **promotion by seniority** and **life-time employment**.

● 一生懸命働けばいいという時代ではなくなっている。

Isshōkenmei hatarakeba ii to iu jidai de wa nakunatte iru.

The days when just **working hard** was enough are past.

● これからは物事を論理的に理解していきたい。

Korekara wa monogoto o **ronriteki-ni** rikai shite ikitai.

We want to look at things **logically** in the future.

● これからの時代、専門知識をもっていない人に
　将来はない。

Korekara no jidai, **senmon-chishiki** o motte inai hito ni shōrai wa nai.

Basically in the future if you haven't got any **special skills** or knowledge you have no future!

3. WHY JAPAN MUST CHANGE
なぜ変わらないといけないか

Having looked at the good and bad sides of the country, we now need to examine the reasons why Japan should change. Forgive a second mnemonic, but the answer lies in the two A's—*America* and *Asia*.

Since the collapse of the Berlin Wall and the end of the Cold War, the curtain has gone up on an age of truly global competition. While Japan once served as the United States ally against communism in Asia, that bogeyman has now vanished. Henceforth Japan cannot expect any special treatment from Uncle Sam. The gloves are off. Cry havoc! and let slip the WTO. Cry tariff! and let slip GATT.

Japan has achieved all that can be achieved as an imitative, mass-production economy. The businesses of the future, the businesses with the high margins are financial services, medical care, and multimedia. Unfortunately in these areas Japan is notoriously weak. If, however, Japan does not manage to catch and ride the wave of new, soft business as deftly as she caught onto electronics in the late fifties, she may, like Britain, embark on a long, slow decline.

The Americans totally dominate software and service industries. New firms are forever springing up there like mushrooms. American firms are meritocracies, unburdened with middle-aged, computer-illiterate middle managers. They encourage and reward risk taking. The nail that sticks out is made company president.

As if that high-end challenge wasn't enough, fellow Asians seem to be muscling into automobiles and semiconductors with a ruthlessness reminiscent of …Japan thirty years ago.

Japan is being caught in pincers, losing out in high value to the Americans, in high volume to the Asians...

Finally for those who like to view things from the historical perspective, Japan changed radically to meet the challenge posed by the industrialized West in the late 1800s. After the war, having seen that militarism led nowhere, she changed again. Now, fifty years having passed, isn't it time for another overhaul of the system. After all, there's no country better at adapting than Japan.

● 今までの日本は恵まれた環境にあった。

Ima made no Nihon wa **megumareta kankyō** ni atta.

Until now Japan was in an unnaturally **lucky** position.

● 戦後50年間、ずっと当り前と思っていた事が一変した。

Sengo gojū-nenkan, zutto **atari-mae to omotte ita** koto ga ippen shita.

Everything that **we took for granted** for fifty years after the war has changed overnight.

● 経済がますますグローバル化しています。

Keizai ga masumasu **gurōbaru [global] ka** shite imasu.

The world economy is becoming more and more **globalized**.

● これからが変革期だと思います。

Korekara ga **henkakuki** da to omoimasu.

From now on we're heading for a **shake-up, a time of change**.

● 量から質への転換。

Ryō kara **shitsu** e no **tenkan.**

The switch from **quantity** to **quality**, from **high volume** to **high value**.

● 労働集約的な産業からハイテク産業へ移行する。

Rōdō-shūyaku-teki-na sangyō kara **haiteku [high-tech] sangyō** e ikō suru.

We want to shift from **labor-intensive businesses** to **high-tech businesses**.

● 今他国がどんどん追い付いてきていますので、日本の独走はもうありえないことです。

Ima takoku ga dondon **oi-tsuite kite imasu** no de, Nihon no dokusō wa mō arienai koto desu.

As more and more countries are **catching up**, Japan can no longer be the only frontrunner.

● 不況もチャンスかもしれません。

Fukyō mo **chansu [chance]** kamoshiremasen.

A **recession** also offers **opportunities**.

- ゆとりのある生活を求めつつある。

Yutori no aru seikatsu o motome-tsutsu aru.

People are insisting on **more leisure time.**

- 成熟した市場においては、売上高ではなく、**利益率**の
向上という方向では進めなくてはいけない。

Seijuku shita shijō ni oite wa, uri-agedaka de wa naku,
riekiritsu no kōjō to iu hōkō de susume nakute wa ikenai.

From now on the big thing is not to increase our turnover,
but our **profitability.**

4. ACKNOWLEDGE THE NEED FOR CHANGE
方向転換の必要性を認める

Despite Japan's obvious strengths, after examining the evidence
of weakness within the country, and the pressure from abroad,
the conventional wisdom concludes that a country that is not
evolving is degenerating, and, like the shark that perishes if it
ceases to swim forward, the absence of progress spells death!
This section, unlike the others, deals not in reasons to change,
but in different ways of expressing the conclusion that change
is *inevitable.*

While the language in this section may appear commonplace to the point of triteness, I would contend that to the Japanese, a phrase such as "We must run with the spirit of the age"

has a peculiar resonance, and "If we don't catch this wave" is more than just pseudo-Californian MBA-speak. Why? Because the Japanese are conscious that the prosperity of their country as a whole is based upon global preeminence in a relatively small number of industries (automobiles, electronics, optics) which they piled into in the late fifties when they still had the advantage of a weak currency, low labor costs, and friction-free access to the American market.

In consequence of the rapid growth of these industries, the major companies involved grew enormous, and enormously diversified. Panasonic, which we in the West think of as only as a manufacturer of audio equipment, in fact produces white goods, personal computers, mountain bikes, and houses. The Toyota group, which we think of as a car manufacturer, also produces trucks, builds houses, and runs an international telephone company.

Having seen companies grow from nothing to something colossal in only a few decades, and experienced a trickle-down effect of Niagaran proportions, has rendered the Japanese more conscious than Europeans, certainly, of how one technological wave can serve to enrich communities, even an entire country.

One can see that while the Japanese maintained their run of luck, catching the semiconductor wave (Kyocera, NEC), and the video-game wave (Nintendo, Sega), it is the Americans who are now monopolizing the PC/Internet wave with firms like Microsoft, Compaq, and Sun Microsystems all swelling from nothing to dominate the New York stock exchange within a few years of their founding.

● 歴史をたどっていけば…

Rekishi o tadotte ikeba…

If we look at the **lessons of history**…

● 国際化が進んでいる背景に…

Kokusaika ga susunde iru haikei ni...

Against a background of ongoing **internationalization**...

● 世の中の変化が激しい。

Yo no naka no **henka** ga hageshii.

Things are **changing** fast and furiously.

● このマーケットは曲がり角に来ている。

Kono maaketto [market] wa **magari kado** ni kite iru.

The market has reached a **watershed**, a **turning point.**

● 世の中に合わせていかないとダメ。

Yo no naka ni **awasete ikanai** to dame.

If we don't **adapt to the changes** taking place,
we won't survive.

● 波に乗れないと…

Nami ni **norenai** to...

If we don't **catch this wave**...

● 時流に乗る。

Jiryū ni noru.

To seize the **zeitgeist**/Be in tune with the spirit of the age.

● 21世紀をにらみながら…

Nijūi-seiki o nirami-nagara…

As we look towards the **twenty-first century**…

5. HOW TO ACHIEVE CHANGE
日本こう変わるべきだ！

This section can be summed up simply as the application of the lessons learned in sections 2 and 3.

If companies have become excessively bureaucratic, conservative, and hierarchical, their traditions must be turned on their heads. While not ditching the old values of "Let's all pull together," creativity, individuality and originality must be encouraged. Merit will be recognized in employees regardless of age or sex. Asahi beer's successful "After 9" black beer was the brainchild of a young woman still in her twenties. Palette Plaza, a fast expanding franchise photo-development shop has a boss still in his early thirties. Future Pirates, one of Japan's most successful computer game design firms which produced a CD-ROM based on Hanna Barbera's *Wacky Races*, is run by the baseball-capped 32-year old Tsuyoshi Takashiro. More and more companies are introducing nonpermanent project teams, and performance-related pay. One can now, as it says on stock advertisements since the stock market crash of 1987, "go down as well as up" within an organization. Some companies, obviously hoping to work on the individuality problem from the outside are introducing a casual day on Fridays.

Therein lies the crux of the problem. The Japanese are used to identifying problems and solving them systematically, locating areas of weakness and strengthening them methodically. With roads, steel production, and automobiles everything is measurable, progress can be seen to be happening. But how does one measure individuality? One cannot foster it by the will of the Keidanren, nor introduce it by government decree. This is what is, perhaps, hard for the Japanese to deal with. Individuality may be the result of a degree of benign neglect, of haphazardness. It is not, unfortunately, something that can be acquired by rote, however hard one tries.

Just as it is widely felt that individuals should be given freer rein within the group and diversity must be encouraged, so it is beginning to be felt that companies should cease to be sprawling conglomerates which diversify into every area their competitors have diversified into, regardless of whether it is a core competency or not. Specialization has dethroned diversification.

● 意識改革を起こさないと…

Ishiki-kaikaku o okosanai to…

We've got to bring about a revolution in people's way of thinking, a total **change of mindset**…

- 個性尊重というマインドに切り換えないと
  そろそろアブナイ。

Kosei-sonchō to iu maindo [mind] ni kiri-kaenai to
sorosoro abunai.

We've go to change to a culture that respects the **individual**
soon *or else*!

- 周囲に左右されず、自分なりに考え、行動を
  起こすことが必要です。

Shūi ni sayū sarezu, **jibun-nari-ni** kangae, kōdō o okosu
koto ga hitsuyō desu.

It's important to not be influenced by other people's opinion,
but to **think and act for yourself.**

- 独自性をもつ会社を目指す。

Dokujisei o motsu kaisha o mezasu.

We've got to become a company with
originality and **flair**.

- 成長の唯一の道は消費者のあたらしい
  ニーズをさぐることです。

Seichō no yui-itsu no michi wa shōhisha no **atarashii
niizu [needs]** o saguru koto desu.

The only possible route to growth is to search out
new consumer needs.

● インターネット時代は英語が使いこなせないとダメ。

Intaanetto [internet] jidai wa eigo ga tsukai-
konasenai to dame.

In a world with the Internet, if you can't speak English
you're no use to anyone.

● アジアを中心に置いた政策を展開していきたい。

Ajia [Asia] o chūshin ni oita seisaku o tenkai shite ikitai.

We want to put **Asia** squarely at the center of our
global operations.

6. THE CHANGE MUST BE JAPANESE STYLE
路線変更は日本的でないといけない！

This last section is small but significant. Yes, change is essential
for survival, but the character of that change must not be shal-
low, greedy, selfish, and socially divisive, in short it must have
none of the faults traditionally ascribed to capitalism by social-
ists. It must be a soft, quasi-seasonal change. Not a robber
baron change, but a benevolent patriarch kind of a change. It
must be a subtle fusion of American values and Japanese values, in which, while the ends are the same—the monopoliza-
tion of markets, the development of saleable products—the
means have all their sharp edges rounded off. Thus, while the
American corporation elbows its way to success, the Japanese

corporation bounces lightly forward, like some zephyr-blown beach ball floating horizonwards.

In addition to this alloy of East-West values, the Japanese will always insist that their strategy for the future is filled with *dreams* and *hopes*. While American bosses interviewed in *Forbes* and *Fortune* will indulge every opportunity to rant megalomaniacally about *their own* vision for *their own* company, the Japanese vision of the future is far less Hitlerian, tending to veer more towards a full-employment Utopia than a 1000-year Reich of downsizings and offshore production. The ultimate aim of the company is to benefit society, not to provide the shareholders with higher and higher dividends.

If we take a quick look at a few company slogans we can see just how prevalent the dream theme is:

ShinNitetsuKagaku is obliging enough to use an English slogan: *For your dreams and happiness.* Nomura Securities, meanwhile, has the slogan: 夢を支える力でありたい *We want to have the strength to support your dreams.* (The cynic might be tempted to ask if this refers to the practice of compensating gangsters for stock losses).

Reiku, a loan company, uses the slogan **"Yume-mirai-hon-bono"** which can be translated something like *Dreams–The Future–Warm and Sentimental.* This, one feels, describes more aptly the sentiments of the lender than those of the borrower.

As stated elsewhere, the Japanese are not much disposed to sarcasm, thus automobile companies, despite their lavish contribution to greenhouses gases, can claim unmocked to be acting *"for the earth itself."* Construction companies can urge us to *"love the earth more,"* while mining companies can claim to be *"head over heels in love with the earth"* (The relationship has, obviously, passed the penetrative stage...)

Company songs again insist on similar themes of hope, brotherhood, dreams, and a better future. The employees of Ito-Yokado group *"holding hands, fly forth into the world with mighty hope,"* Obayashi-gumi employees yearn, it seems, *"to carve out dreams on the earth,"* while Toyota claims to *"make history with a global dream."*

● 日本特有の**協調主義**を合わせ持った個人主義を目指したい。

Nihon-tokuyū no **kyōchō-shugi** o awase motta kojin-shugi o mezashitai.

I want to aim for a combination of Western individualism that retains the Japanese sense of the **importance of the group**.

● 夢のある戦略を展開していきたい。

Yume no aru senryaku o tenkai shite ikitai.

I want to pursue a strategy based on an **idealistic vision!**

● 数字より大切なものがあります、それは日本人の心。

Sūji yori taisetsu-na mono ga arimasu, sore wa **Nihonjin no kokoro**.

There's something more important than the **numbers**, and that is... **Japaneseness**.

11 Furuki yoki analog-jidai

Suzuki: Mukashi wa yokatta na. Washi mo hachimaki o maite, kono te de kikai o tsukutte itan' desu yo.

Masuda: Maa, wareware **Nihonjin wa mono-zukuri ga tokui** da kara.

Suzuki: Ima wa, Ajia [Asia] to no kyōsō ga taihen da. Hontō-ni **chō-kyōsō jidai** dana.

Masuda: Sore o nori-kiru tame ni, yori **furekishiburu [flexible]-na kōzō** o mezasanai to...

Suzuki: Saikin kono kaisha wa nan da ka kōchoku shite iru to omowanai?

Masuda: Maa, Nihon de wa, **nan demo pataan [pattern-] ka shite shimau'n desu yo.** Kono **soshiki mo mōo chotto Amerika-teki** dattara ii na to omotte itan'desu.

Suzuki: Amerika-teki to iu to? **"Wa" o taisetsu ni suru shūdan-shugi** wa aru teido made wa subarashii koto da to omou kedo...

Masuda: Yahari, **jōhōka-shakai ni haitte kara, yo no naka no henka ga hageshiku narimashita.** Ima made no wareware no ichiban tsuyokatta haado [hard] no bunya ga, tei-kosuto [cost] no Ajia [Asia] no hoka no kuniguni ni itte shimatte, wareware wa fukakachi no takai sofuto [soft] o kaihatsu shinakute wa ikenai no desu.

Suzuki: **Amerika no sofuto [soft] wa sugoi** na. Mukō no shōhin ga sekai-ichi na no wa kesshite gūzen ja nai. Nihon ni kurabete, **dokujisei, sōzōsei o sonchō suru shisutemu [system] ga kicchiri dekite iru** shi, **gakureki ya nenrei de wa naku, kojin o sonchō suru seido mo dekite iru.**

Masuda: **Ima no Nihon no wakai hitotachi ni, yaru ki wa nain' ja nai desu ka?**

Suzuki: Iiya, tada **hitori-hitori ga jibun no sōzōsei o hakki dekiru kankyō** ga dekite nai dake da.

Masuda: Sō desu ne. Korekara, **21-seiki ni mukete, Nihon-tokuyū no "wa" to Amerika tokuyū no sōi o hitotsu ni shita shafū** o tsukutte ikimashō.

古きよきアナログ時代

Suzuki and Masuda are in reflective mood and are discussing the company's past and how it will face the challenges of the future. How are they to deal with the twin challenges of competition from low cost Asian hardware manufacturers and high quality American software producers? Read on!

スズキ： 昔はよかったな。わしも八巻を巻いて、この手で機械を作っていたんですよ。

マスダ： まあ、我々日本人は、物作りが得意だから…

スズキ： 今はアジアとの競争が大変だ。本当に超競争時代だな。

マスダ： それを乗り切るために、よりフレキシブルな構造を目指さないと…

スズキ： 最近この会社は何だか硬直していると思わないか。

マスダ： まあ、日本では、何でもパターン化してしまうんですよ。この組織ももうちょっとアメリカ的だったらいいなと思うことがあるんですよ。

スズキ： アメリカ的と言うと？「和」を大切にする集団主義は、ある程度までは、素晴しいことだと思うけど…

マスダ： やはり、情報化の時代に入ってから、世の中の変化が激しくなりました。今まで我々の一番強かったハードの分野が、低コストのアジアのほかの国々に行ってしまって、我々は付加価値の高いソフトを開発しなくていけないのです。

Those Good Old (Analog) Days

鈴木電気の昔を懐かしく思う鈴木社長と増田さんですが、時代と共にアメリカ的経営が尊重される風潮に鈴木電気の将来を重ね合わせています。鈴木電気は今後どのような経営を行うべきなのでしょうか。日本の伝統的な経営、あるいはアメリカの効率的な経営、それとも和洋折衷の経営でしょうか。

Suzuki: I miss the good old days, when I used to wrap a scarf around my head and actually make the machines myself.

Masuda: Well, **we Japanese do like making things**…

Suzuki: Yes, but now the competition from Asia's really hotting up. It really is "**The age of mega-competition.**"

Masuda: In order to face down that challenge, **we've got to aim for a more flexible company structure**.

Suzuki: Don't you feel the company's got kind of rigid and bureaucratic lately?

Masuda: Well, **in Japan everything ends up being systematized, conforming to a pattern.** To be honest, I *have* thought it wouldn't be a bad thing if **this company were a little bit more American in style**.

Suzuki: What exactly do you mean by American? Personally, I think that preserving harmony is—up to a point—an excellent thing.

Masuda: Yes but, **since the information society took off, the pace of change is breathtaking**. The hardware business, that used to be our strongpoint, has basically moved over to Asia, and we've no choice but to come up with some high value-added software.

スズキ：　　　アメリカのソフトはすごいな。向こうの商品が世界一なのは決して偶然じゃない。日本に比べて、独自性、創造性を尊重するシステムがきっちりできているし、学歴や年齢ではなく、個人を尊重する制度もできている。

マスダ：　　　いまの日本の若い人たちに、やる気はないんじゃないですか？

スズキ：　　　いいや、ただ一人一人が自分の創造性を発揮できる環境ができていないだけだ。

マスダ：　　　そうですね。これから、21世紀にむけて、日本特有の「和」とアメリカ特有の創意を一つにした社風を作って行きましょう。

Suzuki: That American software is really amazing stuff. You know it's not just luck that their products are world-beaters. I mean, compared to Japan, they have **a system which values originality and imagination. They respect the individual himself, not the college he went to, or how old he is!**

Masuda: **But young people nowadays. They don't** *want* **to work...**

Suzuki: No, I disagree. **They need an environment where they can be creative.**

Masuda: I guess you're right. **As the twenty first century approaches, let's aim to create a company culture that mixes our own values of harmony with American-style creativity.**

• Mukashi 昔

For all the myths of the painless triumph of the Japanese economy, many small manufacturers who began their working lives in the late 1950s now find themselves bewildered by the pace of change. They long for the old days when work was something done by men in grubby workshops, not machines in gleaming factories. Suzuki is feeling nostalgic about this simpler period when work was work, and the complex influences of the global economy did not need to be taken into account.

It is frequently said of the Japanese that they enjoy work *per se*, and do not do not regard it just as a means to be able to enjoy leisure. Work, they feel, is their birthright, and they cannot understand why currency dealers should wish to deprive them of it. As an example of this, see Akio Morita's biography *Made in Japan* (see chapter entitled "World Trade, Averting Crisis") in which he waxes indignant about fluctuations in the value of the yen as if it were not an inescapable economic phenomenon, but some wicked piece of trickery designed to prevent honest craftsmen doing a good day's work. This simple view of work, as a healthy natural urge to be enjoyed, rather than some dread burden—festering with residual prejudices against capitalist exploiters—to be borne is one of the most striking, healthy and imitation-worthy features of Japan.

When Adam was expelled from Eden, God told him he would have to live by the sweat of his brow. This, presumably, was intended as a punishment. The Oriental Adam, however, put on his *hachimaki*, prevented his brow from sweating, and thus, outwitting the supreme being, contrived to enjoy his toil!

• Wareware 我々

This pronoun has an impressive ring to it, and should be used when you are speaking on behalf of your company. Something like the royal "we" it has an importance-inflating effect. It is very frequently used in the combination **Wareware Nihonjin...** "We Japanese." But surely not all 120 million Japanese are the same?

• The Mega-competition Age   超競争時代

This phrase is found in Sakaiya Taiichi's *Taihenna Jidai* (a pun on **taihen**—"terrible," and **taihen**—"big change") a bestseller from 1995, that put forward the (by now) conventional view that everything the Japanese have taken for granted since the end of the war, no longer holds good. It is worth noting that change is considered a bad thing in Japan. Consider the greeting, "**Kawari wa arimasen**" (There is no change.)

• Wa   和

This word that means *harmony, reconciliation, unity,* significantly also means *Japanese,* as in *wasshitsu*—a Japanese-style room, *waei*—Japanese-English.

• Fukakachi   付加価値

Moving up the *value-added* ladder is something the Japanese have been doing consciously for decades. Witness Toyota's move from textiles into trucks in the thirties, from trucks into passenger cars in the fifties, and their move up to luxury cars with Lexus in the late eighties.

• Amerika-teki   アメリカ的

Ironically, while Americans struggle to understand what it is that makes the Japanese so successful by reading books like *The Kaisha* (James C. Abegglen and George Stalk Jr.), the Japanese in turn read prodigious quantities of American-authored books on management. Whether anyone learns anything or not, plenty of books are sold. That's business!

• Mukō   向こう

Gaijin, or "outside people," appear to live in a place no more geographically definite than "over there." This lack of precision may be a consequence of **sakoku** (1539–1853), the period when Japan was closed to the outside world, and one was literally here or there, inside or outside.

• Gakureki　学歴

Note the word—Gakureki-shakai, a society in which one's status is determined by one's school record.

• Soft　ソフト

In Japanese, **soft** refers not merely, as in this instance, to computer software, but to all non-hard products. Thus, movies, management consulting services, and magazines can all be classified as "**soft**." Without subscribing to the view that the Japanese exaggerate their financial problems and over-emphasize their weakness in software and services in order to lull the rest of the world into a sense of false security that will enable them to move into and dominate more and more economic sectors, the conventional wisdom that the Japanese are no good at soft things is simply not true. Computer games is a field absolutely dominated by Nintendo, Sega, Namco, and Sony, while Japanese comic books and animated films (*Power Rangers*, *Dragon Ball*) are hugely successful all over the world.

• Ima no wakai hito　今の若い人

This reactionary lament about the laziness of today's youth is taken up in unusual quarters. Ohmae Kenichi, former head of McKinsey Japan and the great proselytizer of logic, reason, and the American way (see Chapter 10), informs us in one of his books that his barber in Marunouchi used to be only busy at lunchtimes, evenings, and on the weekend, but that now the degenerate, modern salaryman is found getting a haircut on weekday afternoons.

• 21-seiki ni mukete　21世紀にむけて

Such epic levels of pomposity are best left to those in the upper ranks.

物知り英語ノート

• Making things

この "物作り" という日本人の好きな決まり文句は日本の新聞の社説によく登場します。このように頻繁に使われる決まり文句は **Old chestnut**（古いクリ）と呼ばれます。

• Hotting up

同じように **Getting more intense、Growing fiercer**（より激しくなる）を使うことができます。海外で生活をしたことのない一般の日本人は、国外で韓国のメーカーと日本のメーカーが激しく競い合っていることに気付かないのではないでしょうか？ ロンドンのピカデリーサーカスでは日本企業の看板のすぐ横に韓国のサムソンの大きな広告看板が設置されていますし、ダイウーは昨年英国で12,000台もの車を販売したという事実があります。台湾の低価格コンピュータ、エーサの勢いを見ても分かるように、アジア各国との競争はますます激しくなるでしょう。

• The age of mega-competition

堺屋太一氏の著書にも出てくる "超競争時代" という言葉ですが、もっと英語らしい言い方をしたい場合には **An age of extremely fierce、global competition** と言えます。**Mega-** という接頭語は **Megabrand**（主流ブランド）のように良く使われます。

• To face down

"問題に直面しその問題を解決する"

• Rigid and bureaucratic

フレキシブルな会社を目指す現代において、この "硬くて官僚的" という意味を持つ言葉は変革対象のキーワードとなっています。

• Conforming

"他と一致する、他からはずれないように同化、均一化する" 一般的に日本人は **Conformist**（順応者、法律・慣行に従う人）だと言われています。反対語は **Non-conforminst** です。

• To be honest… a little bit

日本人は強く相手を批判しないと言われますが、英語の世界においても同様に、批判を柔らかくするために **a little bit** のような言葉を使用します。

• Up to a point

"ある程度まで" お茶を濁す時に便利な表現です。

• Strongpoint

反対語は **Weak point** だけでなく、日本語でも致命的な弱点を表わす時に使う **Achilles' Heel**（アキレスけん）があります。

• Stuff

意味のはっきりとしない漠然とした言葉を使っています。ご注意下さい。（Chapter 3参照）

• Amazing

同じ意味に **Awesome**、**Incredible** があります。

• College

アメリカでは日本ほどの学歴社会が構築されていませんが、やはりアイビーリーグカレッジを卒業した学生の就職率、就職先はよいでしょう。日本の著名な起業家や現在コンピュータ業界で活躍する若い経営者の多くは大学中退、もしくは大学へ進学しなかった人が目立ちます。（Chapter 10参照）

• Young people nowadays

この決まり文句を口にすると "このオヤジは偏屈だ" と思われてしてします。ご注意を！

• Harmony and creativity

最後に増田部長が提案したのは、**A compromise solution**（妥協解決）です。ここでは調和を大切にする日本式経営と創造性を重視するアメリカ式の中間に位置する解決策となっています。

TEN

●

MYTHS, LEGENDS, & HEROES OF THE JAPANESE BUSINESS WORLD

日米ビジネス界の伝説の登場人物

The world of business in each country has its own myths and legends, gods and heroes. We in the West are all familiar with the time-management of Benjamin Franklin, the epic ruthlessness of the turn-of-the-century "robber barons," the benevolent paternalism of Thomas Watson Sr. and Jr., and the whiz kids and "instantaires" of Silicon Valley. But whom does the salaryman admire, and aspire to resemble? Who populates the Japanese business Olympus? Who are the Dale Carnegies, the Henry Fords, and the Bill Gates-es of Japan? What is the Japanese business-bible equivalent to *In Search of Excellence*, and who wrote it?

This chapter, in answering such questions, aims to provide you with the same *frame of reference* as your Japanese counterparts, and enable you to make insider allusions and comparisons appropriate to every situation.

1. GREAT JAPANESE ENTREPRENEURS
日本の企業家

We have selected as our archetypal entrepreneur-heroes the following three personages—Konosuke Matsushita (Matsushita Electric), Soichiro Honda (Honda Motors), and finally Akio Morita (Sony). They neatly cover the whole entrepreneurial spectrum, with Matsushita as the frugal, hardworking quintessentially Japanese *arbeitgeber* clawing his way up from poverty and misfortune to grand old man of industry-dom; with Honda as the rough diamond, unconventional, uncouth, but an innovative genius; and Morita as the urbane and cosmopolitan philosopher-king of modern Japanese industry.

KONOSUKE MATSUSHITA—松下幸之助

● 松下電器の最初の工場は、松下さんが住んでいた
狭い畳部屋であった。

Matsushita Denki no saisho no kōjō wa,
Matsushita-san ga sunde ita semai
tatami-beya de atta.

Matsushita Electric's first factory was the cramped
tatami-room where Matsushita lived.

● 進んだ経営の考え方を学ぶため、松下さんは昭和26年に
　　アメリカへ行きました。

Susunda keiei no kangaekata o manabu tame,
Matsushita-san wa Shōwa nijū-roku-nen ni
Amerika e ikimashita.

In order to study advanced management Matsushita
went to America in 1951.

● 昭和32年、小僧から立身し、成功した日本の復活の
　　シンボルとしてタイム誌の表紙に載せられた。

Showa sanjū-ni-nen ni, **kozō kara risshin shi, seikō
shita Nihon no fukkatsu no shinboru [symbol]**
to shite TAIMU [TIME]-shi no
hyōshi ni noserareta.

In 1957 he was featured on the cover of *Time* as **someone who
had fought their way up from being a mere apprentice to
become the symbol of Japan's recovery.**

SOICHIRO HONDA—本田宗一郎

● 昼間は会社で金をもうけて、夜は芸者を引き連れて
　　本田さんは遊びまくった。

**Hiruma wa kaisha de kane o mōkete, yoru wa geisha o
hiki-tsurete** Honda-san wa asobi-makutta.

**By day he made money at the firm, but by night he used
to paint the town red with his band of geisha girls.**

● 戦争のあと、尺八を吹き、お酒を飲んで、次に
　　やることを一年間ぐらい考えていました。

Sensō no ato, shakuhachi o fuki, o-sake o nonde, tsugi ni
yaru koto o ichinenkan gurai kangaete imashita.

After the war he spent about a year playing the Japanese flute
and drinking, just thinking, about what to do next.

● 「良品に国境なし」は、本田さんの前向きな
　　スローガンだった。

"Ryōhin ni kokkyō nashi" wa, Honda-san no maemuki-na
surōgan [slogan] datta.

Honda's positive slogan was **"Quality goods know
no frontiers."**

● 会社に大切なのは夢と若さを保つことだ、と本田さんは
　　信じていました。

**Kaisha ni taisetsu na no wa yume to wakasa o tamotsu
koto da**, to Honda-san wa shinjite imashita.

Honda believed that **it was important for a company to stay
young and never lose sight of its dreams.**

AKIO MORITA—盛田昭夫

● 最初から、盛田さんと井深さんの方針は、時代に
   先駆けた製品を造ることだった。

Saisho kara, Morita-san to Ibuka-san no hōshin wa, **jidai ni
saki-gaketa seihin** o tsukuru koto datta.

Right from the start Morita and Ibuka's intention was to create
products that were ahead of their time.

● ソニーは「電子産業界のモルモット」と呼ばれていました。

Sony wa **"denshi-sangyōkai no morumotto"** to
           yobarete imashita.

Sony used to be called **"The Guinea Pig of the
Electronics World."**

● アメリカの証券市場に日本企業として初めて株を
   上場したのはソニーだった。

America no shōken-shijō ni **Nihon-kigyō to shite hajimete**
kabu o jōjō shita no wa Sony datta.

The first Japanese firm to get a listing on the New York Stock
Exchange was Sony.

● ソニーは今でも家庭的主義経営を目指しています。

Sony wa ima demo **katei-teki-shugi-keiei** o
           mezashite imasu.

Even now Sony is still aiming for **family-style management.**

2. JAPANESE HISTORICAL FIGURES
戦国時代の武将

Sherlock Holmes always referred to his archenemy Moriarty as "the Napoleon of crime," and the Japanese enjoy making similarly grandiloquent comparisons between present-day businessmen and the great warlord leaders of Japan's past. Casually toss in a reference to one of them and you will be the insider of insiders, a chorus of "Sugoi, ne! Hontō-ni Nihon no koto o yoku shitte imasu yo ne!" ("You know everything about Japan") can be guaranteed!

The Japanese businessman likes to compare himself to great leaders from Japanese history, particularly from the **Sengoku Jidai** (The Warring States Period—1467–1587). This may be because it is not decorous to compare yourself with someone living, or only recently dead (particularly if from a competitor keiretsu), but more, I think, because remote historical personages are a more perfect, purer expression of the virtues they represent. Without thought of self or self-enrichment, they toiled for the weal of the country. That is the ideal!

This list explains what qualities and characteristics the three main figures of this period (Nobunaga, Hideyoshi, and Ieyasu) typify.

Nobunaga Oda (1534–1582)

- was the son of a warlord, thus he is the **elite type**.

- introduced a new policy to establish free markets and free guilds, thus he is the **entrepreneur type**.

- used modern tactics (i.e. guns) in warfare and is thus the **technophile type**.

Hideyoshi Toyotomi (1536–1598)

- Came from a family of farmers and is thus the **archetypal self-made man**.

- Took care of people around him better than Nobunaga (who occasionally slaughtered women and children) and is thus the **caring manager type**.

- Prosecuted the Christians thus is the **anti-degenerate foreign influence type**.

- Held on to power too long and is thus the archetype of the **boss who doesn't know when he should make way for new blood**.

Ieyasu Tokugawa (1542–1616)

- introduced a new policy to divide society into a rigid hierarchy, thus he is the **archetypal bureaucrat**.

- paved the way for three centuries of peace, thus he is the **wise and noble leader type**.

as expected

● やっぱり、あの人は国際マインドをもっているから、信長型ですね。

Yappari, ano hito wa kokusai-maindo [mind] o motte iru kara, **Nobunaga-gata** desu ne.

I guess that in so far as he's internationally-minded, **he's the Nobunaga type**.

● あの企業家は新しいことに挑戦して、まるで信長の
　　　　現代版ですね。

Ano kigyōka wa atarashii koto ni chōsen shite, marude
Nobunaga no gendaiban desu ne.

The way that entrepreneur tries new things he's like
a modern day Nobunaga!

● 農民から立身出世した秀吉は、やはり成り上がりの
　　　　典型ですね。

Nōmin kara risshin-shusse shita Hideyoshi wa, yahari
nariagari no tenkei desu ne.

Hideyoshi, who rose from being a mere farmer, is the
archetype of the self-made man.

● 士農工商制度を導入した家康は、現在の日本を牛耳って
　　　　いる、何にでも口を出したがる官僚の
　　　　　　前兆として考えられます。

Shi-nō-kō-shō-seido o dōnyū shita **Ieyasu** wa, genzai no
Nihon o gyujitte iru, nan ni de mo kuchi o dashitagaru
kanryō no zenchō to shite kangaeraremasu.

Ieyasu, who introduced the rigid divisions of samurai-farmer-
artisan-merchant into Japanese society can be thought of as **the
forerunner of the modern civil servants** who try to control
absolutely everything.

3. GREAT WESTERN ENTREPRENEURS
欧米の企業家

In Japan the individual entrepreneur is less important than the company in which innovation and experimentation have been institutionalized. The heroic pathfinder figure is almost an irrelevance. Nonetheless worrying about the absence of young, inventive, risk-taking businessmen is—as we saw in the previous chapter—one of the classic bits of salaryman small talk. We provide a list of people worth worrying about!

In order to spur themselves on to ever higher and higher levels of economic excellence the Japanese love to deluge themselves with bracing showers of information on American entrepreneurs. While the Europeans chose to compensate for their inability to compete with the United States economically by affecting an irritating pose of cultural and moral superiority, the Japanese enjoy challenging the industrial Goliath. Following the dictum "Know thy enemy," the Japanese press is full of news on American business and entrepreneurs. And whereas the Western reader of *Forbes* or *Fortune* (The *Penthouse* of the Plutocracy) will only drip with dreamy money-lust as he devours the glossy photos of besuited men and the vital statistics of their salaries and stock-options, the Japanese reader will have a more practical interest in the technological challenge or opportunities that the individual *represents*. Of course, some of the noise surrounding American entrepreneurs in Japan reflects nothing more than the power of the American media (*Time*, *Newsweek*, CNN) which tends to focus on Americans.

It is worth noting that since Japan began its modernization drive in the Meiji era it has had an almost pathological tendency to measure itself against other countries. While this expresses itself in endless lists of statistics comparing square meters of parkland per urban resident, average life expectancy, salary and so forth, it also has a less scientific outlet in rather facile, general comparisons. In this tradition, one function that the gaijin entrepreneur has is to serve as a rhetorical tool. Masayoshi Son, entrepreneurial founder of SoftBank, a (highly acquisitive) software distribution company can be neatly encapsulated and explained as the "Bill Gates of Japan." Fujitsu can be described as the "IBM of Japan." Mr. Mori, property tycoon and one of Japan's richest men, as "The (less loud-mouthed) Donald Trump of Japan."

In extreme contrast to the Japanese salaryman whose ultimate success in life may well be (pre)determined by which university he gets into and which company he joins, the American entrepreneur is enviably free to make his own destiny. He can drop out of university, raise venture capital, float his company, and amass huge sums of money at an age when his Japanese equivalent is working overtime for peanuts and living in some dreary suburban dormitory. This puts foreign business information in the same bracket as violent or erotic comic books—things that have no relation to the salaryman's drab, everyday existence but in vicariously satisfying his desire to assert himself, provide a cathartic safety valve.

On a more serious note, many of the entrepreneurs best-known in Japan are active in areas in which Japan is traditionally weak such as airlines (Richard Branson), software (Bill Gates), direct selling and customization (Michael Dell, Ted Waitt) and discount retailing (Sam Walton).

- ヴァージンのリチャード・ブランソンみたいな
  風雲児は日本にいない。

Vaagin [Virgin] no Richard Branson mitai-na fu-unji wa
Nihon ni inai.

In Japan there are no *enfant terribles* like Virgin's
Richard Branson.

- アメリカ人の企業家が強く思われている一つの原因は、
  不動産業界のトランプ氏みたいに、皆
  自己PRがうまいからです。

Amerika-jin no kigyōka ga tsuyoku omowarete iru hitotsu no
gen'in wa, fudōsan-gyōkai no Trump-shi mitai-ni, mina
jiko PR ga umai kara desu.

One reason that American entrepreneurs are thought of as all-
powerful is that they're so **good at self-publicity** like the
developer Trump.

- ダイエーの中内氏はウォルマートのサム・
  ウォルトンの日本版だよ！

Daiei no Nakauchi-shi wa Uorumaato [Walmart] no **Sam
Walton no Nihon-ban** da yo!

Daiei's Nakauchi is **Japan's answer to Sam
Walton** of Walmart!

● マサヨシ・ソンのことは、よく第二のビル・ゲーツ
　　　　として騒がれている。

Masayoshi Son no koto wa, yoku **dai-ni no Bill Gates** to
shite sawagarete iru.

Masayoshi Son is frequently raved about as **"the second
Bill Gates."**

*sawagu
make a fuss*

● 終身雇用制のうみの親は日本人ではなく、IBMの創立者
　　　ワトソンさんではないでしょうか？

Shūshin-koyōsei no umi no oya wa nihonjin de wa naku,
IBM no sōritsusha Watson-san de wa nai deshō ka?

Surely **the father of lifetime employment** isn't anyone
Japanese but Thomas Watson Sr., the founder of IBM?

● 大学を中退したアメリカ人の企業家は少なくない。
　　　例えばマイケル・デルそれとビル・ゲーツ…

Daigaku o chūtai shita Amerika-jin no kigyōka wa sukunakunai.
tatoeba Michael Dell sore to Bill Gates…

There are quite a few American entrepreneurs who **dropped
out of university**, for example Michael Dell and Bill Gates.

● ボディ・ショップの創立者ロディックさんによると、
　　　経営に必要なのは情熱だ！

Bodi-shoppu [Body Shop] no sōritsusha Roddick-san ni
yoru to, **keiei ni hitsuyō na no wa jōnetsu da!**

According to The Body Shop founder, Anita Roddick, **what is
really necessary for management is enthusiasm, passion!**

4. JAPANESE BUSINESS WRITERS
日本のビジネス・ライター

It is not our intention to provide a comprehensive bluffers guide to Japanese business writers. We have merely selected five of the best-known and the sentences on the opposite page teach you how to refer to them in passing.

STOCKMARKET GURUS

Appropriately enough in a stockmarket where most of the trading is done by foreign investors (Japanese shares being held to a far greater extent by corporations as tactical cross shareholdings rather than by profit-hungry individuals) the leading two writers in Japanese on the Japanese stockmarket are both foreign.

Richard Ku is a Chinese-American who was born in Japan. After a spell as a banker in the United States he joined the Nomura Research Institute whence he now pontificates. His comments can be found regularly in all the newspapers.

Peter Tasker is the head of the Japanese branch of Kleinwort-Benson, a British merchant bank, in Japan. He has written a number of books in Japanese on the collapse of the bubble economy and frequently appears as a commentator on TV. On his books' bellyband blurb he is somewhat grandiloquently called **Gendai-no-yogensha** or the prophet of the present day.

OTHER GURUS

Sakaiya Taichi is a graduate of Tokyo University and worked for MITI before retiring in his early forties to concentrate on writing. He is thus a classic **elite course o susunda hito.** Highly prolific, he has produced salaryman and historical novels as well as works on socioeconomic trends and management. Since he can put a historical perspective on things, his view of the present is felt to be both more profound and more *Japanese* than that of say, Ohmae Kenichi.

Tanaka Naoki is yet another graduate of Tokyo University who has written widely on the Japanese economy and politics.

Ohmae Kenichi was until recently head of McKinsey, the American consulting firm, in Japan. We could thus call him "The Tom Peters of Japan" (**Tom Peters no Nihon-ban**). Although he always castigates Japanese companies for rushing to produce identical products to their competitors and creating profitability-destroying over-supply, he blithely goes on producing two books plus infinite magazine articles every year with no apparent fear of saturating the market.

Obviously aware of the old saying "No man is a prophet in his own country," Ohmae-san purveys Japanese wisdom in the US and American wisdom in Japan. In the late eighties his book *Borderless World* achieved considerable international success. He himself appears to believe in the *borderless book* concept, as after reading a number of his works, one gets the impression that the same chapters are merely leaping around and rearranging themselves in a different order from book to book.

Since he completed a graduate degree at MIT, is married to an American citizen, and worked for a US company, he is regarded as a bit **Butter-kusai** (smell of butter, over-westernized). His style of writing is considered un-Japanese since he is logical, hard-headed, and outspoken in his criticism. This, however, does make him popular with salarymen who regard themselves as a little radical and *avant-garde!* His Japanese books are western thoughts expressed in Japanese and are good to read if you wish to learn how to say what you are really thinking in Japanese, rather than metamorphose into a yes-man zombie.

- リチャード・クーが指摘したように、円高の原因の
  大半は日本側にある。

Richard Ku ga shiteki shita yō ni, endaka no gen'in no
taihan wa Nihon-gawa ni aru.

As Richard Ku pointed out, the greater part of the responsibility for the high yen is to be found on the Japanese side.

- ピーター・タスカが言ったように、平成不況下で日本経
  済のさまざまな構造的問題が表面化した。

Peter Tasker ga itta yō ni, Heisei-fukyōka de Nihon-keizai
no samazama-na kōzō-teki mondai ga hyōmenka shita.

As Peter Tasker said, the Heisei recession has brought a lot of
structural problems of the Japanese economy to the surface.

= IRO IRO

- 堺屋太一が書いたように、日本は峠を超えたと
  実感している人が多い。

Sakaiya Taichi ga kaita yō ni, Nihon wa tōge o koeta to
jikkan shite iru hito ga ooi.

As Taichi Sakaiya wrote, there are many people in Japan
who now who feel the country is past its peak.

to realize

- 田中直毅の言葉を借りると、最近日本の
  創造性が枯れ始めた。

Tanaka Naoki no kotoba o kariru to, saikin Nihon no
sōzōsei ga kare-hajimeta.

To borrow a phrase of Naoki Tanaka, recently Japan's
creativity has begun to dry up.

- 大前研一によると、日本の会社はどこも同じ商品を
造ることに殺到し、過当競争になって、
だれも儲からない。

(handwritten: everyul g everyu)

Ohmae Kenichi ni yoru to, Nihon no kaisha wa dokomo onaji shōhin o tsukuru koto ni sattō shi, katō-kyōsō ni natte, dare mo mōkaranai.

According to Kenichi Ohmae, the reason no one makes any money in Japan is that all manufacturers rush to produce the same products creating excessive competition.

---

5. AMERICAN BUSINESS WRITERS
西洋のビジネス・ライター

Basically the same books on management that cause a stir in the West also cause a stir in Japan. As we pointed out in Chapter 4, many key American management concepts such as the エクセレント・カンパニー (excellent company) and リエンジニアリング (reengineering) have made the crossover into the Japanese language. This indicates that the book from where they come have been widely read. I have selected Tom Peters, Michael Hammer, and Peter Drucker as our representative triumvirate of management mandarins.

IN SEARCH OF TRANSLATABLE EXPRESSIONS

Tom Peters' first book *In Search of Excellence* was written to inspire America's managers wilting in the face of the Japanese challenge. Recently his sales in Japan have been bolstered by linking him with fellow McKinseyian Ohmae Kenichi who allegedly "oversees" the Japanese translations of his works.

Given his propensity for jargon and elaborate metaphors, referring to Tom Peters in passing may not be advisable. After all, off the top of your head, can you give me the Japanese for "the vigorous pursuit of serendipity," the "adhocracy," "simultaneous loose-tight properties," "chunking," "anti-NIH pills" etc?

REENGINEERING ROBOCOP

While at the height of the bubble economy in the late 1980s, America was viewed as a land in which vulture-like lawyers and greedy, unprincipled, overweight managers lorded it over a populace of illiterate, gun-toting, AIDS-infected crack-heads, the US high-tech revival has created a renewed respect for American business. In 1989 *Robocop* might have been taken as a portrait of America as it was, but now the States are felt to be represented by Bill Gates, Andy Grove, and Marc. L. Andreesen. It appears to be "morning in America," thus a prescriptive and practical book, like **Michael Hammer's** *Reengineering the Corporation*, rather than a merely anecdotal and demagogic, albeit inspiring one (No offence, Tom!) is likely to appeal to Japanese businessmen worried about losing the competitive edge.

HIGH PRIEST OF THE DISMAL SCIENCE

Drucker, the father of management, needs no introduction. Personally I find it hard to respect someone who is so lavish in his praise of Japanese education. As Van Wolferen pointed out, the original meaning of the word educate is "to bring forth and develop the powers of the mind," not "to produce a docile and dehumanized workforce."

● トム・ピーターズが言ったように、エクセレント・
　カンパニーの一つの特徴は社員が皆仕事が
　　　　最高に楽しいと信じ込むことだ。

Tom Peters ga itta yō ni, ekuserento-kanpanii [excellent
company] no hitotsu no tokuchō wa shain ga mina
shigoto ga saikō ni tanoshii to shinji-komu koto da.

It was Tom Peters who said that one of the characteristics of
the excellent companies is that the employees
really enjoy their jobs.

*believe
completely*

● トム・ピーターズが書いたように、激変期に入ったら、
　　合理経営を捨ててよりゆるやかな組織を
　　　　　目指すべきである。

Tom Peters ga kaita yō ni, gekihenki ni haittara, gōri-keiei
o sutete yori yuruyaka-na soshiki o mezasu-beki de aru.

Tom Peters was right when he said that in a time of dramatic
change one must abandon rational management and aim for a
looser, fuzzier organization.

should

● マイケル・ハマーの言葉を借りると、ほとんどの
　　欧米の会社は二世紀前からの原則に従って
　　　　　経営を行っている。

Michael Hammer no kotoba o kariru to, hotondo no Ōbei
no kaisha wa niseiki mae kara no gensoku ni shitagatte
keiei o okonatte iru.

To use Michael Hammer's phrase, European and US
businesses are running their companies according
to a set of principles laid down two centuries ago.

- ピーター・ドラッカーが指摘したように、日本が こんなに速く経済大国になったのは優れた 教育制度のおかげだった。

Peter Drucker ga shiteki shita yō ni, Nihon ga konna ni hayaku keizai-taikoku ni natta no wa sugureta kyōiku-seido no o-kage datta.

As Peter Drucker has pointed out, the reason Japan rose to be an economic giant quite so fast was thanks to the excellent education system.

12 Kigyōka no "yoku"

Watanabe: Suzuki-shachō ga daigaku o dete inai ni mo kakarawazu, jibun no doryoku de kyodai-na kigyō o tsukuri-ageta no wa, hoka no sengo no ookina kigyōka to no kyōtsūten desu ne.

Masuda: Sō desu ne …Matsushita Kōnosuke, Honda Sōichirō nado, seishiki-na kyōiku o ukezu ni, subete o genba de mananda oo-mono ga nan-nin ka imasu yo ne.

Watanabe: Eriito [Elite] to iu yori shokunin-katagi deshita ne.

Masuda: Sō desu yo! Yahari, ano sedai wa mina kosei ga tsuyokatta ne. Hontō-ni shigoto ga daisuki de, isshō-kenmei ni ganbatte imashita.

Watanabe: Nee. Ima no wakamono wa nan ka zenmai-jikake no ningyō mitai desu kara ne.

Masuda: Shachō no kosei wa tokidoki attō-teki datta kedo. …Kōjō ni kite, rain [line] de hataraite iru hito ni baka-yarō to donattari, yopparatta toki, geisha o mado kara nage-dashitari to itta yō na koto wa chotto…ne.

Watanabe: Ore wa, soko ga suki da! Kaisha o sodateru chikara o motsu hito de areba, sono enerugii [energy] ga afurete, iron-na hakeguchi o hit-suyō to suru no wa atarimae no koto da yo.

Masuda: Sō sō, hakeguchi no hanashi de omoi-dashitan da kedo, uwasa ni yoru to shachō no o-mekake-san wa go-nin iru-rashii.

Watanabe: Kaisha no zenseiki ni wa sō datta kedo, saikin wa san-nin ni hetta. Kedo toshi no sa o kan-gaetara sōtō no mono da. Ichiban wakai ko wa tatta no jūkyū-sai da yo!

Masuda: Yappashi, keizaigaku no kyōkasho ni notte inai gensoku ga arun da. "Kigyōka no sōzōsei to seiyoku wa hirei shite iru" to iu....

Watanabe: Dō ka na? Uchi no baai sono gensoku ga hataraite inai ne, nikuyoku ga afurete iru no ni, watashi ga setsuritsu shita McVitie-sha wa nakanaka seichō shinai.

Chuck: Nihongo de "sexism" wa nan to iimasu ka?

Watanabe: Urusai! Omae wa Seiyōjin da kara, Nihon no yuniiku [unique]-na bunka o rikai dekinai dake da yo!

企業家の「欲」

Watanabe has become friends with Masuda in the course of his consulting work at Suzuki Denki. Here they discuss the character of Suzuki and compare him to other great Japanese entrepreneurs. They speculate about the entrepreneur's creative (and other) urges.

ワタナベ：　鈴木社長が大学を出ていないにもかからわず、自分の努力で巨大な企業を作り上げたのは、他の戦後の大きな企業家との共通点ですね。

マスダ：　そうですね。松下幸之助、本田宗一郎など、正式な教育を受けずに、全てを現場で学んだ大物が何人かいますよね。

ワタナベ：　エリートというより職人気質でしたね。

マスダ：　そうですよ！やはり、あの世代は皆個性が強かったね。本当に仕事が大好きで、一生懸命に頑張っていました。

ワタナベ：　ねえ、いまの若者はなんかぜんまい仕掛けの人形みたいですからね。

マスダ：　社長の個性は時々圧倒的だったけど。工場に来て、ラインで働いている人にばかやろうと怒鳴ったり、酔っ払った時、芸者を窓から投げ出したりといったようなことはちょっと…ね

ワタナベ：　おれは、そこが好きだ！会社を育てる力を持つ人であれば、そのエネルギーがあふれて、いろんなはけ口を必要とするのは当り前のことだよ。

The Entrepreneurial "Urge"

鈴木電気の増田さんと意気投合した渡部さんが、鈴木社長の性格は
日本の偉大な起業家とよばれる松下幸之助や本田宗一郎に通ずると
ころがあると指摘しています。偉業を成し遂げる人とは性欲にあふ
れているのが条件？

Watanabe: The fact that Suzuki built up a huge company by
his own efforts despite not going to university is
something he shares with other great entrepreneurs of the postwar era.

Masuda: Hmm… yes. There are quite a few people like that
who had no formal education but learned everything hands-on in the field. Think of Sōichirō
Honda or Kōnosuke Matsushita.

Watanabe: They're more the artisan or craftsman type than
the technocratic elite.

Masuda: That's definitely true. People of that generation
had tremendously strong characters. They loved
their work and they worked incredibly hard.

Watanabe: Young people nowadays are just like clockwork
automatons.

Masuda: Mind you, the boss's character was sometimes
overwhelming. He would come to the factory and
call people working on the assembly line "son of a
bitch," and when he was drunk he used to throw
geisha girls out of windows. That's a little… well,
you know.

Watanabe: I really like that! It's inevitable that if a man has
sufficient drive to create a business, he's over-
flowing with energy, energy which has to express
itself, work its way out somehow.

マスダ： そうそう、はけ口の話で思い出したんだけど、うわさによると社長のおめかけさんは五人いるらしい。

ワタナベ： 会社の全盛期にはそうだったけど、最近は3人に減った。けど年の差を考えたら相当のものだ。一番若い子はたったの19才だよ！

マスダ： やっぱし、経済学の教科書に載っていない原則があるんだ。「起業家の創造性と性欲は比例している」という…

ワタナベ： どうかなあ？うちの場合その原則が働いていないね、肉欲があふれているのに、私が設立したマクビティー社はなかなか成長しない。

チャック： 日本語で sexism は何といいますか？

ワタナベ： うるさい！おまえは西洋人だから、日本のユニークな文化を理解できないだけだよ！

Masuda: By the way, talking about letting off steam, rumors say that the boss has five mistresses.

Watanabe: He did—when the company was doing really well—but recently the number's fallen to a paltry three. Mind you, if you look at it in terms of age difference it's pretty impressive. The youngest is only nineteen years old!

Masuda: So then there is an economic law which is not found in the textbooks. *The entrepreneur's creativity is in direct proportion to his physical appetites.*

Watanabe: I wonder... In my case I'm seething with desire, yet McVitie Consulting, the firm I founded, isn't really growing.

Chuck: Excuse me, how do you say "sexism" in Japanese?

Watanabe: Look you're a westerner and you can't understand our unique culture. Now, shut up!

Know-it-all Notes

• Daigaku 大学

Present-day Japanese society is often referred to as gakureki-shakai, a society that judges people by where they went to school. Ladies aspire to marry a 3K boy—someone who combines the desirable qualities of kōgakureki (graduated from a Japanese "ivy-league" college), kōshūnyū (a high income) and se ga takai (tall—the kanji for takai is also read kō). Despite this, the men who created much of Japan's present prosperity such as Sōichirō Honda and Kōnosuke Matsushita were often from poor backgrounds with little formal schooling. Since they had nothing to lose they were prepared to take great risks. They also knew their respective trades inside out. The youth of the present are distinguished by antei-shikō, *a yearning for stability*. This does not produce great entrepreneurs.

A recent article in *Nikkei Business* pointed out how many of the presidents of Japan's most vital, young corporations were people with the guts to "drop out" of university. Examples given included the presidents of game software manufacturers Nintendo and Sega, semiconductor manufacturer Kyocera, and electronics manufacturer Muratec.

• Genba 現場

Literally *the real place*, this means hands-on experience on the factory floor or on sales trips, anywhere but the air-conditioned, chart and figure abstract world of head office. Genba-kankaku, which we can translate as "feel for the product," a "profound knowledge of the business," is an important and respected concept in Japan.

• Elite エリート

Elite course o susunda hito: Those who have attended a top university then entered a top company or government ministry.

Top positions in business and government are almost entirely held by graduates of Tokyo or Kyoto, then Waseda, Keio, or Hitotsubashi Universities. In *The Enigma of Japanese Power*, Karel Van Wolferen provides some statistics that give an insight into just how all-embracing the web of power spun by the elite is. Approximately 70–80% of all section chiefs and bureaucrats of higher rank in the major ministries are from Tōdai. In 1985 the presidents of 401 out of the 1,454 largest firms were Tōdai graduates.

• Kosei ga tsuyokatta　個性が強かった

It is felt, not just by foreign observers, but by the Japanese themselves, that life has become so busy and so competitive, with school, crammer school, part-time jobs, and then an average ten–twelve hour working day, that people have no space left in which to cultivate their individuality. One more extreme view claims that people are so standardized by the education process that they couldn't be individuals even if they wanted to be.

• Shikake　仕掛け

This means *clockwork* or *automatic*. Stanley Kubrick's *Clockwork Orange* is entitled "Tokei Jikake no Orange" (orenji) in Japanese. Watanabe presumably means that young Japanese people now go through their paces, or jump through the hoops, but there is no verve, no enthusiasm, just total subservience to conventionality.

• Baka-yarō　ばかやろう

Baka means something more than simply a "fool." A person who is inept and useless, a baka runs the risk of being cast out of society. Couple with yarō—originally only used to address beasts of burden and later the peasant types who worked them—and you have a phrase that plays on the most undesirable parts of Japanese society and its taboos. As with other languages—consider "bugger" or "bastard" in English—social taboo is the true creator of all obscenity.

These two antics, bellowing at workers and chucking geisha out of windows were specialities of Sōichirō Honda. The geisha—tossed out of a second-floor window in the course of an evening's entertainment—fortunately landed in some electric cables strung along the street and caused a power cut in the neighborhood, but no injury to herself.

• Hakeguchi   はけ口

An outlet. Although, or rather because, the Japanese are generally very repressed and controlled they recognize the need for ways of relieving stress. After toiling at the office it is important to go to the **kanrakugai** (the entertainment district) or **akasen** (the red-light area) and with everything paid for with **settaihi** (entertainment allowance) to **hame o hazusu** (let your hair down) for **stress hassan** (stress relief). After a few drinks one might **abareru** (go wild), then **gero o haku** (puke up) before being stuffed into a taxi paid for with **taxi-ken** (taxi-coupons) and going home to bed.

• Omekake-san   おめかけさん

Should we translate this as *mistress* or *concubine*? Perhaps the latter as the purpose of such women is more for purposes of wealth-display than for passion and romance. The word is rather outdated now, and **aijin** (lover) might be used instead.

Lesley Downer's book, *The Brothers*, about "the richest family in Japan" the owners of the Seibu railway, resort, hotel, and retail empire devotes a lot of attention to the prodigious sexual appetites of the founder, Yasujirō Tsutsumi.

• Urusai   うるさい

Literally meaning "noisy," this word can mean anything from an urgently whispered "be quiet" to a furiously bellowed "shut your mouth." It is amusing to watch a subtitled movie in which "If you don't shut your mouth, I'll blow your fucking head off" is rendered with this single word.

• Unique-na bunka   ユニークな文化

This is a blanket discussion-stopper frequently used (and abused) by the Japanese.

物知り英語ノート

• Hands-on

"実地の"学校で勉強するのではなく、仕事の現場で実際に働きながら技術や知識を吸収していくことですが、日本の偉大な起業家の何人かはこのような体験を活かし大企業を作り上げたといえます。

• Technocratic elite

"技術者出身の政治家"を意味しますが、ここでは現場主義に対して学校で知識を吸収したエリートをさしています。

• Tremendously strong characters

以前に比べると日本人の多くは経済成長とともに、性格的に均一化してしまいました。良い意味でも、悪い意味でも強い個性の持ち主がいなくなりました。

• Call people on the assembly line "son of a bitch"

工場に入って最初に会った人に「ばかやろう」とどなった、という本田宗一郎の実話。

• Throw geisha out the window

芸者を2階の窓から投げてしまったが、運よく電線に引っかかり何事もなく済んだという、これまた本田氏の若き頃の話ですが、本田氏のモットーは Work hard, play hard よく働き良く遊べ！でした。

• Well, you know

まぁ、わかってるでしょ？とはっきり言わずに言葉を濁しています。増田さんはダイレクトに社長を批判することをしたくないので、渡部さんにも会長の行いが多少行き過ぎであることを認めて欲しいようです。同様に You know what I mean も使うことができます。あらためて説明せずともわかって欲しい時に便利です。

• Drive

"願望" ビル・ゲイツの伝記は **"Hard Drive"** ですが、コンピュータのドライブと彼のトップに立ちたいというガンバリズムを表わすタイトルです。

• In proportion to

"比例する"

例：**Wage levels are in proportion to demand for labor**
　　（時給は労働の需要に比例している）

創造力と性欲は比例するという経済学の教科書に載っていない原則に気付いた増田さんですが…エネルギーに満ちあふれている偉大なヒーローたちには2つのタイプがあると言われています。まず、セックスに使わなかったエネルギーを何か目的を達成するために使う性欲昇華型 (**Sublimate sexual energy**)。2つ目は目的のために発揮するエネルギーに負けないほどの性欲を持つタイプです。歴史上の人物では、非常に乱れた生活をしながらもフランスとイギリスを侵略した **Every man's woman and every woman's man**（男のために女になる、女のために男になる）のジュリアス・シーザーが有名です。

• To let off steam

"ストレスを発散する" 蒸気機関車からきている言葉。**To let your hair down** は、髪の毛が垂れるほど「はめをはずす」こと。

• A <u>paltry</u> three

"わずかな" 少ないことを強調する形容詞。

• <u>In terms of</u> age difference

年の差の<u>角度から</u>考えたら。（Chapter 1参照）

例：**Japanese dividends are pitiful, but if you look at stock prices in terms of capital gain, they're not too bad**
　　（日本の配当は雀の涙だが、株を資本利得から考えたらそれほど悪くない）

• You can't understand our unique culture

渡部さんは討論に弱いのでユニーク・カルチャーという逃げの表現をつかっています。

ELEVEN

•

TARZAN IN TOKYO

無言のコミュニケーション

While the decorative and ill-paid office ladies of the Japanese corporation are allowed to leave work at five-thirty prompt, the salaryman is bound by one of Japan's many unspoken laws to stay for at least two or three more hours. Ultimate physical escape from the office only leads to the open-prison of the group drinking session and thence the cattle-train home.

Just as a long-distance runner's brain releases endorphins to kill the pain he feels in consequence of his over-exertion, so the Japanese salaryman exists in a state of permanent "runner's high," ecstatically numb and totally insensitive to fatigue *precisely because he is so tired!*

Of course, with an entire population of "eternal racers" something has to give, and effete Europeans who have forgotten the pleasure to be derived from "a job well-done" (zangyō-jin to shite no mugen no yorokobi) leap with self-righteous *schadenfreude* on any data of broken marriages, of fathers alienated from their children, or of death from overwork as proof that so unbalanced a life as the average salaryman leads is not socially healthy.

Certainly one casualty of the salaryman's battle fatigue is his language. While he may have all the stirring anecdotes, the sonorous commonplaces, and the perfectly nuanced synonyms collected in this book *somewhere in his mind*, they lurk in a part of it that is only activated by the appearance of clients or gentlemen of the press. Everyday communication with colleagues consists of an abundance of pronouns and grunts. The purpose of this chapter is therefore to make you forget everything you have learned so far.

What's good about grunting?

Why should I abuse my Japanese and will I go blind if I do?

- One of the commonplaces of Nihonjinron is that the Japanese can communicate without speaking. We cannot teach you telepathy, but we can teach you sub-verbal communication.

- Being rikkutsupoi (ratiocinative, or an egghead) is generally considered a bad thing in Japan. Speak with grunts and pronouns and you're unlikely to be accused of it.

- When you go out drinking, rather than forget your Japanese and start speaking English, just slide into this Tarzan-speak. It's probably easier than your native language anyway.

- Western Art has progressed from representational cave paintings (stickmen hunting stick animals) to the abstract splatter-fests of Jackson Pollock, or the soothing monochrome canvases of Rothko. Literature has evolved from the linear tales of epic poetry to the seething verbal *bouillabesse* of Burroughs or Ballard. Self-expression tends inevitably towards deconstruction.

    Equally in Japanese you will start off telling simple things as they are (Watashi wa America-jin desu: *I am American*), you will then progress to ostentatious displays of your newly-acquired proficiency (Watakushi wa, Abraham Lincoln to Thomas Jefferson to onaji yō ni, minshūshugi no yurikago de aru Beikoku kara kite orimasu: *I, like Abraham*

Lincoln and Thomas Jefferson hail from the cradle of democracy, the United States), then finally, a **shibui** combination of self-confidence and world-weariness, you will sink into Eastwoodian terseness. (**Ore wa …ko kara kite iru yo**: *I'm from… there*).

13 | Tomita no sōsōkyoku

Tomita: **Aitsura** no sei de ore wa jinin saseraretan desu yo. Naganen ni watatte, kaisha ni hōshi shite kita no ni, jibun no te hitotsu de yakenohara kara takokusekikigyō ni made sodate...

Masuda: Nee, Tomita-san, ochitsukinasai! Suzuki Denki wa Kyōto no kaisha na no de yakenohara nante nakatta deshō! Sore ni kaisha o kizukiageta no wa Tomita-san de wa nakute, Suzuki shachō ja nai desu ka. Chotto toire ni... Shitsurei shimasu....

Tomita: Yappashi, **ano jidai** ga yokatta **na**...

Itō: **Ano jidai tte?**

Tomita: **Shitte ru deshō... rei no...** gaikokujin ga Nihon ni hairenakatta jidai.

Itō: Moshikashitara, Tomita-san wa Edo jidai no sakoku no hanashi o shite irun' desu ka?

Tomita: **Atari mae da yo!**

Itō: Naze totsuzen rekishi no hanashi ni nattan' desu? Tomita-san ga chishikijin da to wa shiranakatta wa!

Tomita: **Aho! Wakaran' ka?** Nihon ga sakoku no mama dattara, ore o kubi ni saseta ano yankii mo koko ni inakatta darō ga?

Itō: Haa... Sō desu ka?

Chuck: Nan no hanashi o shite irun' desu ka?

Itō: **Wake no wakaranai koto bakari itte-te, nanda-kanda to monku o iu kono hito no hanashi,** kiki-akita wa!

Chuck: Seki o kōkan shimashō ka?

Itō: O-negai-shimasu!

Chuck: Kaisha no tame da yo!

Tomita: **Uu... Omae ka!** Ore wa eigo ga nigate da kara, karaoke de mo utaimashō! Karaoke suki?... like sing?

Chuck: Maa... (anata to hanasu yori mashi da yo!)

Tomita: "Dōki no Sakura" shitte imasu ka?

Chuck: Ie, shirimasen. Tomita-san, eigo no renshū no tame ni, Beatles no "Iesutadei" [Yesterday] o utatte mimasen ka?

Tomita: イェスタディ、オール・マイ・トラブル・シームド・ソー・ファー・アエー

富田の葬送曲

Suzuki Denki is set to begin production of the Dream Team PC, and the scene is an expensive hostess bar, where everyone is having a post-project drink. Off stage, however, Suzuki has stepped down and forced arch-parasite Tomita to take early retirement to make way for younger, risk-taking managers like Masuda and Ito. The dethroned Tomita, fueled by whisky and water, is being even more than usually obnoxious and obtuse. But we cannot help but feel pity for him as the curtain falls....

トミタ： あいつらのせいでおれは辞任させられたんですよ。長年にわたって、会社に奉仕してきたのに、自分の手ひとつで焼け野原から多国籍企業にまで育て…

マスダ： ねえ、富田さん、落ち着きなさい！鈴木電気は京都の会社なので焼け野原なんてなかったでしょう！それに会社を築き上げたのは富田さんじゃなくて、鈴木社長じゃないですか。ちょっとトイレに…失礼します。

トミタ： やっぱし、あの時代がよかったな…

イトウ： あの時代って？

トミタ： 知ってるでしょう…例の…外国人が日本に入れなかった時代。

イトウ： もしかしたら、富田さんは江戸時代の鎖国の話をしているんですか?

トミタ： 当り前だよ！

イトウ： なぜ突然歴史の話になったんです？富田さんが知識人だとは知らなかったわ！

Tomita's Swansong

マクビティー社によって提案された新しい会社の方向性に同意した
鈴木社長は、新製品のDream Team PCを生産開始すること、自分
は辞任し新しいことに意欲的に挑戦する若い世代に会社の経営を任
せることを決心しました。もちろん保守的な富田さんにも退職を促
します。意外な展開にショックを受けた富田さんは、ホステスバー
で飲みすぎ同僚やコンサルタントに愚痴をこぼし、しつこくからみ
ます。団魂世代を代表する富田さんの会社生活は悲しく幕を閉じて
いきます。

Tomita: I was made to retire because of **those guys**. I, who for so many years gave my all to the firm, I, who with my own hands built up a multinational business from the smouldering wasteland…

Masuda: Hey, Tomita, don't get carried away! Suzuki Electric's based in Kyoto which wasn't even bombed! Besides the man who built up this company wasn't you, it was Suzuki, Ahem… if you'll excuse me… the bathroom…

Tomita: Oh yes, **those** were the days.

Itō: What days are **those**?

Tomita: **You know what I'm talking about… you know**… the period when foreigners were unable to come into the country.

Itō: Are you perhaps referring to the time when the country was closed up in the Edō period?

Tomita: **Of course I am!**

Itō: Why is it we're suddenly discussing history? I had no idea you were a cultured person!

トミタ： あほ！わからんか？日本が鎖国のままだったら、俺をクビにさせたあのヤンキーもここにいなかっただろうが！

イトウ： はあ、そうですか。

チャック： 何の話をしているんですか？

イトウ： 訳のわからない事ばかり言ってて、なんだかんだと文句を言うこの人の話、聞きあきたわ！

チャック： 席を交換しましょうか？

イトウ： お願いします！

チャック： 会社のためだよ！

トミタ： うう、おまえか！俺は英語が苦手だから、カラオケでも歌いましょう！カラオケ…好き…like sing？

チャック： まあ…（あなたと話すよりましだよ！）

トミタ： 「同期の桜」って知ってますか？

チャック： いえ、知りません。富田さん、英語の練習のために、ビートルズのイエスタデーを歌ってみませんか？

トミタ： *Yesterday, all my troubles seemed so far away…*

Tomita:	**Idiot! Don't you get it?** If Japan were still closed to foreigners now, **that darn American** who got me fired wouldn't have been able to get in, right?
Itō:	*Oh really, Is that so?*
Chuck:	What are you discussing?
Itō:	Tomita-san is talking **a load of nonsense**. I'm sick of listening to his **endless complaints**.
Chuck:	Shall we change places?
Itō:	*PLEASE!*
Chuck:	For God and my… company!
Tomita:	**Urrgh. It's you is it?** I'm useless at English so why don't we sing some Karaoke? You like?
Chuck:	Well… (I guess it's preferable to talking to you.)
Tomita:	Do you know the song "Cherry Trees of the Same Age?"
Chuck:	No, I don't. How about polishing up your English by singing the Beatles' "Yesterday?"
Tomita:	*Iesutadi, ōru-mai-toraburu-shiimudo-sō-faa-awee.*

Know-it-all Notes

- **Yakenohara**　焼け野原

The burnt wasteland. This word used to describe the landscape of cities fire-bombed or atom-bombed by the United States Air Force. Since Kyoto was designated an area of exceptional cultural worth it escaped the bombing, thus for Tomita to claim that he built the company up *from the ashes of a huge bombsite* is just maudlin drunken nonsense.

- **Chotto toire ni**　ちょっとトイレに

Masuda-san avoids open conflict with Tomita by cunningly pretending to hear the call of nature.

- **Sakoku**　鎖国

Literally "closed country" this was the period when Japan—fearful of what had occured in other nations that had invited European settlers, priests, and traders—was closed to the outside world. This state of affairs, which began in 1539, was ended by Commodore James Perry who in 1853 sailed into Yokohama in his Black Ships and forced Japan to sign a trade treaty with the United States. The Black Ships are frequently used even now as an image of foreign pressure (**Gaiatsu**).

- **Atari-mae da yo**　当たり前だよ

Here rather impolite, this has the implication of "of course you fool."

- **Chishikijin**　知識人

"A knowledge person." This rather ungainly word has a companion in the equally stilted **bunkajin**, a culture person. A more attractive word for intellectual would be **kyōyō no aru hito**, while the katakana **interii** provides an easy-to-remember alternative.

- **Ano Yankii**　あのヤンキー

Again this is very insulting in tone and probably accompanied by a toss of the chin towards where Chuck is sitting. A proper translation would be something like "that Yank bastard." Note that the pronoun **ano** is often impolite in tone.

• Sō desu ka　そうですか

Oh really? Itō is here being heavily ironic.

• Kaisha no tame　会社のため

This is an allusion to doing things **o-kuni no tame**, "for the fatherland."

• Nigate　苦手

Tomita must belong either to the generation who were forbidden to learn English (the language of the **Ki-chiku-bei-ei**—Devil-Beast-American-English) during the war, or to the generation who memorized enormous quantities of English grammar but never actually spoke.

　　It is important to recognize that the reason the Japanese are so bad at English is that English exists just as one means for measuring intelligence and for gathering data about young people's abilities. Students shall be despatched to a certain university, thence to a company according to their examination results. English thus exists as a part of the domestic sorting mechanism, not as a living, foreign language.

• Dōki No Sakura　同期の桜

This song, about young Kamikaze pilots going to war and dying like beautiful cherry blossoms, is one of the staples of karaoke and is accompanied by a grainy video of Zeros crashing into American aircraft carriers. Tomita is obviously having a dig at Chuck by trying to make him sing a song about Japanese heroes of World War Two.

• Yesterday　イエスタデー

One of the tiny handful of (exclusively slow and maudlin) western songs found in karaoke in Japan. Other examples would be "The Long and Winding Road," "My Way," and "Heartbreak Hotel." At least in the case of "Yesterday," Chuck will find some consolation in the accompanying video which features a naked woman rolling around in bed. In quite what relation she stands to Paul McCartney's melancholic ballad of love lost is just another mystery closed to those of us who cannot understand Japan's "unique culture."

物知り英語ノート

- **Gave my all to the firm**
"私の全てを会社に捧げた" という日本人のよく使う表現。

- **Smouldering wasteland**
"焼け野原"。ハーレクインロマンスで使われる表現に**Eyes smouldering with passion**（情熱でいぶる目）があります。同じいぶっているものでも**Wasteland**（荒れ地）になると戦後の東京の焼け野原となってしまいます。**On account of changes in the automobile market, and the exodus to the suburbs the center of once bustling Detroit is now an urban wasteland**（自動車市場の変化と、大勢の人々の郊外への移転によって、昔賑わっていたデトロイトの中心街は都会の荒野に変貌してしまった）

- **The Bathroom**
増田さんは富田さんと話し続けることに嫌気がさし、トイレを口実に富田さんから逃れようとしています。

- **Those were the days**
"あの頃はよかった"。古きよき時代 **The good old days** をしのんでいます。

- **I had no idea you were a cultured person**
"あなたが知識人だったとは夢にも思わなかった" とかなり失礼な言い方をしています

- **If Japan were still closed…**
富田さんの理論はうさん臭いところがあります。いまだに鎖国をしていたら、鈴木電気の技術も入ってきていないということになるのですから。このような論理を英語で **Syllogism**（三段論法）といいます。

- **Oh really is that so**
"ああ、そうですか？" と伊藤さんはほとんど富田さんをバカにした口調になっています。

• A load of nonsense
"ナンセンスの塊"。批判するときに使われます。**A load of lies**(うその塊)

• I'm sick of listening to…
"聞きあきた"。同様に **I'm sick and tired of listening to** や **I'm fed up of listening to** を使うこともできます。

• For King and country!
チャックさんは富田さんの隣に座ることになってしまいました。戦いに出る兵士が「王と祖国のために！」と叫ぶような気持ちでしょう。富田さんとの戦いのスタートです。

• I'm useless at English
"英語が苦手です"

例：**Most Japanese are useless at English**
　　（ほとんどの日本人は英語が苦手です）

• Karaoke. You like it?
日本人ビジネスマンの生活に欠かせないもののひとつにカラオケがあります。チャックさんが富田さんの隣に座ることになりますが、チャックさんのコンサルティングによって自分の地位が失われたと信じて疑わない富田さんは、チャックさんへの復讐を思いつきます。死を覚悟しゼロ戦闘機に乗り込む若き特別攻撃隊員が、次々にアメリカ艦隊を目指し大空へと飛び立って行く姿がモニターに映し出される『同期の桜』をチャックさんに歌わせようとします。特攻隊員が捨て身でアメリカ艦隊を攻撃した事実をチャックさんに思い出させ、彼の祖国をばかにしようという考えでしたが、チャックさんにその真意を気付かれ逆に英語の歌を歌わされるはめになってしまいました。

• Yesterday
鈴木電気で頑張った時代を懐かしみ、涙しながら歌う富田さん。

インスタント ビジネス 日英会話
INSTANT BUSINESS JAPANESE

1997年3月6日　第1刷発行

著　者　　ジャイルズ・マリー

発行者　　野間佐和子

発行所　　講談社インターナショナル株式会社
　　　　　〒112 東京都文京区音羽 1-17-14
　　　　　電話：03-3944-6493

印刷所　　株式会社　平河工業社

製本所　　株式会社　堅省堂

英語で話す「日本」Q&A
Talking About Japan Q & A　　　　　ISBN4-7700-2026-0

講談社インターナショナル　編

外国の人と話すとき、必ず出てくる話題は「日本」のこと。でも英語力よりも前に困るのは、日本について知らないことがいっぱいという事実です。モヤモヤの知識をスッキリさせてくれる「日本再発見」の書。

日米比較・冠婚葬祭のマナー
Do It Right: Japanese & American Social Etiquette　　ISBN4-7700-2025-2

ジェームス・M・バーダマン／倫子・バーダマン　著

アメリカでは結婚式や葬式はどのように行われるのか？　お祝いや香典は？……そしてアメリカの人たちも、日本の事情を知りたがります。これだけあればもう困らない。日米冠婚葬祭マニュアル、バイリンガル版。

英語で折り紙
Origami in English　　　　　ISBN4-7700-2027-9

山口　真　著

たった一枚の紙から無数の造形が生まれ出る……外国の人たちは、その面白さに目を見張ります。折るとき、英語で説明できるようにバイリンガルにしました。ホームステイ、留学、海外駐在に必携の一冊です。

英語で読む日本史
Japanese History: 11 Experts Reflect on the Past　　ISBN4-7700-2024-4

「英文日本大事典」編

11人の超一流ジャパノロジストたちが英語で書き下ろした日本全史。外国人の目から見た日本史はどういうものか、また、日本の歴史事項を英語で何と表現するのか。新しい視点が想像力をかき立てます。

「Japan」クリッピング
Views of Japan from The Washington Post Newsroom　　ISBN4-7700-2023-6

東郷茂彦　著

アメリカの世論をリードするワシントン・ポストに書かれた「Japan」……政治、外交、経済、社会のジャンルで取り上げられた日本の姿を、国際ジャーナリストが解説し、その背後にある問題点を浮き彫りにする一冊。

ニッポン見聞録
Heisei Highs and Lows　　　　　ISBN4-7700-2092-9

トム・リード　著

国際化の進む日本ですが、アメリカのジャーナリストが鋭い目と耳で浮き彫りにしたニッポンの姿は、驚くほど平穏で愛おしく、恥ずかしいくらい強欲で無知なものでした。トムが大好きな日本人へ贈る新・開国論。

英語で話す「日本の心」
Keys to the Japanese Heart and Soul

ISBN 4-7700-2082-1

「英文日本大事典」編

一流のジャパノロジスト53人が解説した「日本の心」を知るためのキーワード集。「わび」「さび」「義理人情」「甘え」「根回し」「談合」「禊」「穢れ」など、日本人特有な「心の動き」を外国人に説明するための強力なツールです。

英語で話す「日本の謎」Q&A
100 Tough Questions for Japan

ISBN 4-7700-2091-0

板坂 元 監修

なぜ、結婚式は教会で、葬式はお寺でなんてことができるの？ なぜ、大人までがマンガを読むの？ なぜ、時間とお金をかけてお茶を飲む練習をするの？——こんな外国人の問いをつきつめてゆくと、日本文化の核心が見えてきます。

アメリカ日常生活のマナーQ&A
Do As Americans Do

ISBN 4-7700-2128-3

ジェームズ・M・バーダマン／倫子・バーダマン 著

"How do you do?" に "How do you do?" と答えてはいけないということ、ご存知でしたか？ 日本では当たり前と思われていたことがマナー違反だったのです。旅行で、駐在で、留学でアメリカに行く人必携のマナー集。

ニッポン不思議発見！
Discover Japan: Words, Customs and Concept

ISBN 4-7700-2142-9

日本文化研究所 編 松本道弘 訳

絶望的な場合ですら、日本人は「そこをなんとか」という言葉を使って、相手に甘えようとするらしい……このような指摘をうけると、いかに日本人は独特なものの考え方をしているか分かります。あなたも"不思議"を発見してみませんか。

ビジネスマン必携！

対訳：英語で話す日本経済Q&A
A Bilingual Guide to the Japanese Economy

ISBN4-7700-1942-4

NHK国際局経済プロジェクト・大和総研経済調査部 編

大和総研／NHKの信頼できる情報により、日本経済を英語と日本語のバイリンガルでわかりやすく紹介。楽しく気軽に読める、クイズと会話形式の構成です。